Learning Leadership from Dogs

Learning Leadership from Dogs

What Can Bulldogs, Dachshunds, Komondors, Pekingese, and Otterhounds (Among Other Dogs) Teach Us about Effective Leadership?

Aditya Simha

ANTHEM PRESS

Anthem Press
An imprint of Wimbledon Publishing Company
www.anthempress.com

This edition first published in UK and USA 2025
by ANTHEM PRESS
75–76 Blackfriars Road, London SE1 8HA, UK
or PO Box 9779, London SW19 7ZG, UK
and
244 Madison Ave #116, New York, NY 10016, USA

© 2025 Aditya Simha

The author asserts the moral right to be identified as the author of this work.

All rights reserved. Without limiting the rights under copyright reserved above,
no part of this publication may be reproduced, stored or introduced into
a retrieval system, or transmitted, in any form or by any means
(electronic, mechanical, photocopying, recording or otherwise),
without the prior written permission of both the copyright
owner and the above publisher of this book.

British Library Cataloguing-in-Publication Data
A catalogue record for this book is available from the British Library.

Library of Congress Cataloging-in-Publication Data
A catalog record for this book has been requested.
2024945985

ISBN-13: 9781839990274 (Hbk) / 9781839990281 (Pbk)
ISBN-10: 1839990279 (Hbk) / 1839990287 (Pbk)

Cover Credit: Mike McCartney (https://mccartneysdogs.com/)

This title is also available as an e-book.

I dedicate this book to my beloved wife, Yasaswini, and cherished sons, Advi and Ajinkya for their enthusiastic support of my work, and for their unstinted love for dogs. Both Advi and Ajinkya have being quite possibly the most interested readers of this book. Both of them have also suggested several dogs that I absolutely needed to include in the book one way or the other, and I've done that, which is why the total number of dogs covered in this book has expanded rather prodigiously. And, I should definitely add that both the boys and wife have been mostly willing to go on various dog park or walking or hiking activities with Fiona and I, and that's really helped all of us gain so many rich experiences, meeting new dogs and making new connections.

I also dedicate this book, which is my second book, to Buddy (my darling Red Dachshund) who is probably right now strutting around like a pint-sized toughie in Heaven (where else can dogs go?), and to Fiona (my lovely patient angelic Black & Tan Otterhound. She's definitely the best in the world, and we all love her loads!). I also dedicate this book to all of the other dogs (not owned by me) but with whom I've interacted plenty in my life (Sherry, the lovely black German Shepherd; Ruby, the sweet Black and Tan German Shepherd; Rover, the friendly Dalmatian; Nestor, the placid English Pointer; Zeus, the amazingly clingy and cute Pug; Mona, the delightful Yellow Labrador Retriever; Snowy, the happy Indian Spitz; Buffy, the gentle Basset Hound; Billy, the noble Bloodhound; Louie, the marvelous Clumber Spaniel; Steffi, the lovely Cocker Spaniel; Keto, the lively Yellow Labrador Retriever, and last but not least Monty & Kitty, the two happy-go-lucky Indian Mixed Breeds). I have learned lots from you all, and all of the other dogs I've interacted with throughout my life. You have all made a difference to and improved me as a person.

CONTENTS

Acknowledgments		ix
1.	Introduction to the Book	1
2.	Embody the Bulldog Spirit/Courage	9
3.	(Collie)ty Communication	19
4.	Otterly (O)authenticity	29
5.	Kingly Kindness	41
6.	Rottie Respect	53
7.	Great/er (Dane or Swiss) Gratitude	67
8.	Terrier'izing Trust	79
9.	Inu Intelligence	89
10.	Pe(e)king(ese) at Joie de vivre	103
11.	Ridge(ing) Back to Resilience	115
12.	Setter(ing) Down to a Conclusion	129
Index		135

ACKNOWLEDGMENTS

I have many people to thank and acknowledge, and without these individuals, this book would probably not exist. I will start off by thanking my parents (Anand and Bhramara) for having gotten me my first dog (Buddy), after years and years of me imploring them for a dog, they finally acquiesced to my request. I have to also thank Raghu Uncle for gifting Buddy to me. I must also thank my sister (Aparna) for having helped me with obtaining the various pictures you will see dotted around in the book. I must also thank two of my aunts, and two of my uncles, for having given me dog books, during my childhood, which got me so hooked onto the topic, and I believe my knowledge in this domain exists thanks to those early books, which I obtained. So, thank you very much indeed, Rajashree Aunty and Yogi Uncle, Chitra Aunty, and Gops. Like always, I must also certainly acknowledge my mom for her IRS-like reliability in checking-in-with-me to see how far the book had progressed.

I also thank my various uncles and aunts and other family members, relatives, and friends for having given me an assortment of experiences with their dogs. I would have never have gotten those many experiences with such a wide variety of beautiful dogs. So, thank you so much Raja Uncle & Rukku Aunty, Prasad Mama & Madhavi Aunty, Gops, Venkat, Shrinivas Mama & Sudha Aunty, Molly Cisco, Carol & Gordon Major, Linda & Jeremy Meek, Ashka & Mike Gordon, Sekhar & Uma Enjeti, Goofy Uncle & Madhu Aunty, Raghavan Uncle & Aunty, Dilip Uncle & Shobha Aunty, Teju & Meghana Enjeti, and Sumukh Guruprasad.

My many thanks to my dearly departed paternal (Rajanna and Savitri) and maternal (Dr. Nagabhushan and Vimala) grandparents for being excellent grandparents. I also thank Avinash, Amogh, Ananya, Giri Uncle and Ratna Aunty, Raji Aunty and Prasad Uncle, Sharada Aunty and Pinnu, Kamala Aunty and Shankar Uncle, Ammi Aunty and Rao Uncle, Gopi Uncle and Geetha Aunty, and Chandu Mama for being good eggs.

I also thank my awesome acquisition editor Jebaslin Hephzibah for being so amazingly supportive and so incredibly patient. I asked for several extensions during this book writing process, and she was always so understanding. Thank you so much, Jebaslin, for being so awesome! Thank you also to all of the Anthem support staff for all the help in making this project come to fruition.

Finally, I must thank all the people who I've met through the years and hope to continue meeting more people, who are dog lovers. Dogs are special creatures, who come into our lives and enrich them tremendously—I am glad that that there are so many dog lovers around. The world would be a dull and dreary place without dogs, that's for sure! So, many thanks to the breeders and dog rescuers, who help make the world a better place for dogs and humans alike. Thank you to all my supporters, friends, family, and well-wishers from the bottom of my heart—I have enjoyed writing this book, and I trust you will enjoy reading it, and find it a fun and useful book.

Chapter 1

INTRODUCTION TO THE BOOK

Why Is It Essential to Learn about Leadership?

Unless someone has been rendered comatose and marooned on a deserted tropical island for the better part of two decades, most individuals have a fairly good idea about the importance of leadership. Once our marooned individual finally gets rescued and resuscitated, I would imagine that he or she will immediately grasp the importance of leadership too. On the other hand, you, my gentle reader, probably already know the importance of leadership, especially how essential it is for a person to learn about leadership, and indeed practice effective leadership himself or herself. Why else would you be clutching a copy of this book (or a Kindle unit for the eBook aficionados out there)? Well, it could also probably be due to the Fido factor, but more on that after this early introduction.

Therefore, if for some reason, you need a refresher on the importance of leadership, then this introduction to the book (and indeed the entire book) will serve as one. Leadership is perhaps one of the most valued traits/positions throughout the world, and has invited a lot of attention to it across contexts and disciplines.[1-8] Books, monographs, and articles on leadership are ubiquitous—a Google, a DuckDuckGo, or a Bing search will reveal millions of results on the topic of leadership. There are hundreds of institutes and universities worldwide that have programs or courses on leadership. Some journals exist primarily to showcase scholarly articles on leadership (e.g., *Leadership Quarterly*, *Journal of Leadership Studies*, *Leadership*, etc.). And of course, there is no real or artificial shortage of leadership book titles either. Many books on leadership exist, and this current volume is one in that number. I myself have written one of those books (that book uses a Harry Potter context to explain leadership).[9] However, there is one aspect that is unique to this book—I allude of course to the canine context, which I have juxtaposed with the leadership context.

Hmm[…] it is also likely that you are a dog lover, as many folks around the globe tend to be. Perhaps, the title of the book caught your attention, and why wouldn't it, after all? So many alluring dogs in the title itself. Let me now explain a little bit more in detail about why I have chosen to write a leadership book enveloped by a canine context around it. The answer is simple—I believe that the domestication of dogs is probably one of the best things that has ever happened to humankind. I absolutely love and adore dogs, of all spots, patches, and stripes, and have spent an inordinately large number of years studying and learning about the various dog breeds out there. I've had experience with dogs from childhood on, and I suspect I will be retaining my fondness for dogs up until the moment when the Grim Reaper arrives for me with scythe unsheathed. Anyway, on to the how and what we can learn from our canine friends, especially as it pertains to leadership.

How and What Can We Learn from Dogs?

Dogs have been helping humankind since at least 15,000 years now, at least if historical and anthropological research can be believed.[10,11] In the early days, dogs were used primarily to help with protection duties and assist with hunting expeditions. Those two duties still exist, of course, but many others have been added on with the passing of time and the advancing of civilization. Seeing-eye dogs, therapy dogs, drug-sniffing dogs, military dogs, among others, are all occupations that our early ancestors could not have imagined (or they did, and there is a cave painting somewhere in some yet-to-be-discovered cave, lovingly created by an early Picasso).

Anyhow, the fact that so many dogs assist us and help us with so many of our tasks can help provide a sense of how important dogs are to us. I am sure that folks who dislike dogs will demur at this statement (yes, regrettably, there are a lot of people who seem to dislike dogs, some perhaps with genuine reason), but they too cannot deny the enormous contributions that our canine friends make for us. From an economic perspective, just consider folks who are in the business of farming livestock (or we could say Farmers, but a bit of specificity never hurt anyone). Without livestock protection breeds (e.g., the Anatolian Shepherd, the Tibetan Mastiff, the Great Pyrenees, etc.) to guard their livestock from predators, these farmers could potentially see immense losses in their livestock.[12-14] The same applies for herding dogs like Collies, German Shepherds, Australian Shepherds, and so on. These dogs provide an invaluable service for farmers, and the benefits of that service are not just restricted to economic benefits but also for mental well-being.

From a mental health and emotional well-being point of view, I would argue that the benefits of having pet dog companions are priceless. They have therapy dogs for a reason—in my own institution, during exam week, we have therapy dogs who are made accessible for students.[15] This helps reduce their stress levels significantly, and I personally always enjoy going up and saying my hellos to these stress-buster squad members. Additionally, for visually challenged

INTRODUCTION TO THE BOOK

3

individuals, having a seeing-eye dog (such as a Labrador Retrievers and Golden Retrievers) is phenomenally invaluable for letting them lead independent lives. People suffering from post-traumatic stress disorder (PTSD) also benefit tremendously from just having stress-busting dogs as pets.

Now that I have briefly touched upon the importance of dogs for us, I will discuss how and what we can learn from our four-legged furry (well, mostly furry, except for the Xolo or the Crestless and some other hirsute-challenged breeds, of course) friends. Or to be more specific, I will layout in this chapter what lessons this book is going to cover in terms of what we can learn from dogs. Different breeds have different traits and different temperaments, and differing historical purposes as well. I believe that we can learn specific attitudes and behaviors from these various dogs and use that information to improve and impact our own leadership skills and styles.

I must mention that most of the information discussed in this book will be based on what we know as "recognized pure-breed dogs." By recognized, I mean that a specific breed is recognized by some sort of Kennel Club, be it the American Kennel Club (AKC), The Kennel Club (the UK version), or the KCI (Kennel Club of India), which means that I will not be referring to some of the designer breeds that are very popular today (e.g., the Cavapoos, Goldendoodles, PugFinlands, etc.). This is not due to some inherent bias against designer breeds or cross-breeds but is more because we have a lot of evidence (historical and current) about the temperaments and predilections of established pure-breed dogs. After these current designer breeds become more established and their temperaments are more or less stable, then perhaps a future version of this book will incorporate those breeds as well. Basically, I would predict that today's designer breeds may turn out to be tomorrow's purebreds. But in this current edition, I am going to focus on the more established and recognized breeds. So, if you are eager to read about and learn from ChiRish WolfHuaHuas or PugOndors, you may be needing to wait a while.

However, please know that if you do not have a purebred dog of your own, you can still learn many things from your pet, regardless of what breeds may be in your pet's ancestral lineage. So, please don't go getting upset that this book is seemingly slighting your dog—that is not my intention at all. A pet dog, regardless of its lineage, is a beloved and amazing dog. Go give yours a hug! I am only using purebred dog breeds in this book because it makes it easier for me to describe their traits and utilize the history behind the development of the breed, as I explain how that matters for leadership. I will also not be able to cover or feature every single breed of recognized purebred dog out there—this book is not going to rival *War and Peace* in terms of length (the word count for that worthy volume is 587,287 words!). Although, I'm not sure that even Tolstoy could have managed to feature every single breed of

4 LEARNING LEADERSHIP FROM DOGS

dog in his magnum opus. Similarly, I will not be covering every single concept or theory in leadership in this book, including theories of followership, which have gotten rather prominent in recent times. But every chapter in this book focuses on concepts that consider the importance of followers for leaders.

Structure of the Book

Now, I will discuss the essential structure of the book. Your eye has perhaps gone to the (clever, as per me) catchy titles of the various chapters. That was done intentionally, of course. A pun or two never hurt anyone, did it? So, after this first chapter, the rest of the chapters will revolve around the central themes of the lessons that I believe we can learn from dogs. In total, I am aiming to have twelve chapters in this book. While I could write another one to make it a Baker's dozen, but while I am not suffering from triskaidekaphobia myself, some readers might, so to avoid triggering any trauma, let us stick to twelve chapters.

The second chapter of this book will focus on the broad theme of courage. Think about it, leaders need to be courageous. Who is going to want to follow a pusillanimous leader? Not many would! In the courage chapter titled "Embody the Bulldog Spirit/Courage," I will of course refer to the wonderful Bulldog, but I will also describe many other breeds who exemplify an unfailing courage. I will also discuss some ways by which leaders (and followers) can increase their own reservoirs of fortitude. Yes, it can certainly be done—how, well, you'll need to peek ahead at Chapter 2 for that.

The third chapter of this book will focus on the broad theme of communication. Could we hope to work well with a leader who never communicates? I would guess not. While dogs cannot speak in human tongues yet, their communication strategies are pretty well-developed and easy to decipher. This chapter is titled "(Collie)ty Communication," and as the title signals, the chapter will discuss a lot on shepherd dogs of various descriptions, including the Rough Collie, which happens to be a firm favorite of mine. I will discuss ways by which you can improve your own communication skills, be it verbal or nonverbal.

The fourth chapter of the book will focus on the broad theme of authenticity. This is one area of leadership that has gotten a lot of attention this past decade, and it does not appear that the attention is waning anytime soon. This chapter is titled "Otterly (O)Authentic," first because of alliterative preferences, as I firmly believe that alliteration makes the world go whirlingly. But more seriously, because the Otterhound is one amazingly beautiful shaggy dog and absolutely exemplifies authenticity. I will, of course, also describe and discuss other dogs pertinent to this theme. In this chapter, I will discuss ways by which individuals can become authentic leaders themselves.

INTRODUCTION TO THE BOOK

In the fifth chapter, the theme that will be discussed is kindness. While the chapter is titled "Kingly Kindness," the truth is that any other dog breed could have effortlessly been attached to the word. In this chapter, I will discuss why kindness is an essential trait to aim to emulate and will especially talk about how kindness is necessary for facets of organizational justice. In this chapter, I will also discuss ways by which individuals can become kinder individuals, and why that is an important trait for them to consider honing and improving. As always, I will discuss and describe some specific dog details that pertain to the central theme of the chapter.

The sixth chapter will focus on respect. Yes. R-E-S-P-E-C-T, with a hard-sounding R. This is another quality that leaders certainly need to possess. Establishing a culture of respect is one duty that leaders must try to set. It works that way with dogs too—far too often, fights among dogs boil down to some misunderstanding based on disrespect. In this chapter titled "Rottie Respect," I will discuss ways by which leaders can be respectful as well as get their followers to be respectful.

The seventh chapter will focus on gratitude. That quality is one that can have immense beneficial consequences for all concerned. People receiving it tend to feel happy, while people feeling it tend to have a sense of equanimity. It is a great quality to focus on, and thus, the chapter is titled "Great/er (Dane or Swiss) Gratitude." In the chapter, I will discuss the importance of gratitude and how one can focus on improving one's receptivity toward gratitude. Almost every single dog out there espouses a sense of gratitude, unlike their feline cousins, who normally don't (except for Siamese cats usually, but let's not get distracted talking about cats—this is a dog-based book, after all). So, this chapter will be all about gratitude.

The eighth chapter will focus on the theme of trust. The chapter is titled "Terrier'izing Trust" and is a play on the fact that the chapter features loads of Terrier dogs in it. Trust is a quality that leaders need to engender in themselves and in their followers as well. Without trust, there is not much a leader can really do. In this chapter, I will discuss ways by which you can become trusted as well as trusting. You need a bit of both, after all! It's just like how when we trust our dogs, our dogs trust us right back!

The ninth chapter is going to focus on intelligence, in the aptly named "Inu Intelligence." In this chapter, I will discuss the various dog breeds that exemplify the concept of intelligence (all major forms of it), and additionally, I will discuss how individuals and leaders can improve their own levels of intelligence. The "Inu" in the title refers to dog in the Japanese language, and the title just plays off on that—it's also a bit of a spoiler because you know you're going to read about the Shiba Inu in the chapter.

6   LEARNING LEADERSHIP FROM DOGS

I am happy to report that the tenth chapter will focus on happiness, and specifically is titled "Pe(e)king(ese) at Joie de vivre" (which is French for exuberant joy). Without joy in life, individuals will face dreary existences. Leaders too can hardly hope to have happy employees or followers, if they themselves are the morose kinds. I will discuss some of the various dog breeds that exemplify this exuberant joy for life and discuss how leaders can themselves embrace joy and establish a culture of joy and happiness.

The eleventh chapter titled "Ridge(ing) back to Resilience" will focus on grit aka resilience. Failure and setbacks are part and parcel of life, and leaders need to be able to bounce back from failure. Resilience is perhaps one of the most important qualities out there—only if you try again after facing failure, can you ever hope to taste success. Like other chapters, this too will include a discussion of some of the dog breeds that are incredibly resilient.

The twelfth chapter is titled "Settering Down to a Conclusion," and as the title suggests is a concluding chapter for this book. In this chapter, I will essentially summarize the contents of the various preceding chapters and provide you with tangible takeaways that you can obtain from the overall book.

So, that's pretty much what the layout of the book is going to be. As you can espy from the above short descriptions, the various leadership themes I will be focusing on in this book center around themes such as trust, courage, kindness, and so on. And, of course, I will be introducing and detailing some of the lessons that various dog breeds can offer us. While I have chosen these various breeds, you do have to understand that the list of dogs is in no way all-encompassing or complete. I have simply chosen some of the dogs that came to my mind—to yours, you may think of something entirely different. People who love dogs (like yours truly) will I think especially enjoy the book; however, that is not to say that people who don't like dogs would not learn anything from the book. They too will learn from the book; it's just that they may not enjoy it as much as their canine-loving compatriots will, or maybe they will after they glimpse a sight of dogs in photographs. The next chapter will focus on courage, and I will discuss the why's and how's and what's on courage.

Summary

This chapter is basically the start of the book, where I present information on how the book is to be laid out. I have introduced the themes and titles of each of the subsequent chapters, and I intend for the reader to gain a good perspective of both leadership concepts as well as the various dog breeds described in the book. So, let's muster up our intestinal fortitude and bustle along to the next chapter, on courage.

References

1 Antonakis, J., Banks, G., Bastardoz, N., Cole, M., Day, D., Eagly, A., ... & Weber, R. (2019). The leadership quarterly: State of the journal. *The Leadership Quarterly*, 30(1), 1–9.
2 Bass, B. M. (1985). Leadership: Good, better, best. *Organizational Dynamics*, 13(3), 26–40.
3 Casimir, G., & Waldman, D. A. (2007). A cross cultural comparison of the importance of leadership traits for effective low-level and high-level leaders: Australia and China. *International Journal of Cross-Cultural Management*, 7(1), 47–60.
4 Kaiser, R. B., Hogan, R., & Craig, S. B. (2008). Leadership and the fate of organizations. *American Psychologist*, 63(2), 96.
5 Kanji, G. K. (2008). Leadership is prime: how do you measure leadership excellence? *Total Quality Management*, 19(4), 417–427.
6 Lowe, K. B., & Gardner, W. L. (2000). Ten years of the leadership quarterly: Contributions and challenges for the future. *The Leadership Quarterly*, 11(4), 459–514.
7 Outhwaite, S. (2003). The importance of leadership in the development of an integrated team. *Journal of Nursing Management*, 11(6), 371–376.
8 Zimmermann, P., Wit, A., & Gill, R. (2008). The relative importance of leadership behaviours in virtual and face-to-face communication settings. *Leadership*, 4(3), 321–337.
9 Simha, A. (2022). *Leadership Insights for Wizards and Witches*. Emerald Group Publishing: Leeds, England.
10 Morey, D. F., & Jeger, R. (2015). Paleolithic dogs: Why sustained domestication then? *Journal of Archaeological Science: Reports*, 3, 420–428.
11 Savolainen, P. (2007). Domestication of dogs. *The Behavioural Biology of Dogs*, 21–37.
12 Arnott, E. R., Early, J. B., Wade, C. M., & McGreevy, P. D. (2014). Estimating the economic value of Australian stock herding dogs. *Animal Welfare*, 23(2), 189–197.
13 Wilkes, R., Prozesky, H. E., Stannard, C. G., Cilliers, D., Stiller, J., & Whitehouse-Tedd, K. (2023). Recruitment and satisfaction of commercial livestock farmers participating in a livestock guarding dog programme. *Journal of Vertebrate Biology*, 72(23029), 23029–23031.
14 Hall, S., Dolling, L., Bristow, K., Fuller, T., & Mills, D. S. (2016). *Companion Animal Economics: The Economic Impact of Companion Animals in the UK*. Oxfordshire, UK: CABI.
15 https://events.uww.edu/campus-events/event/5932-pet-therapy.

Chapter 2

EMBODY THE BULLDOG SPIRIT/COURAGE

What Is Courage?

Before embarking on a journey by ship, it is after all vital to understand where the ship is sailing to. If one aims to go to Tibet, it would hardly be worth the effort to sail to Tasmania. Similarly, unless we truly know what courage stands for, it would be a bit odd to delve into an entire chapter on the topic. Most people would define courage with a synonym—some would say that courage stands for bravery or fortitude. But those are not definitions! I would define courage as a quality that allows a person to willingly pursue a course of action that could be risky, but the person does it anyway because there is a purpose behind that action.

The title of this chapter pretty much provides what the end journey is going to be.

Indeed, I will focus on courage, and talk about some dog breeds that absolutely reflect courage. While the title suggests that I will be spending a major chunk of this chapter relating the exploits of Bulldogs, today's modern Bulldog does not bear a whole lot of similarity with its earlier ancestors. The Bulldogs of yesteryear were used for bull baiting (a cruel sport), which has luckily been outlawed since.[1-4] Ever since, Bulldogs have more or less become cute charismatic Churchillian dogs. However, the expression "Bulldog Spirit" while frequently used to talk about tenacity, can also apply to courage. Think about it—Bulldogs were used to bait Bulls, who are much larger animals. That itself speaks volumes about the courage aspect inherent in Bulldogs. In this chapter though, apart from the Bulldog, I will focus on discussing several livestock guardian dog breeds, who are renowned over the world for their courage.

Courage is something that humans could do to improve themselves. Far too often, you will see leaders (and followers, it must be said) wilting under strenuous or high-pressure circumstances. They lack the courage to do the right thing, and they often end up behaving in ways that are contrary to how they ought to. Think about the individuals who agree to engage in unethical activities just because their supervisor or boss tells them to. Similarly, think

10   LEARNING LEADERSHIP FROM DOGS

about the individuals who fail to take the right action, just because they are scared of someone else or scared of possible unpleasant consequences. Imagine a situation where a city police officer declines to give an offender a speeding ticket, just because that offender is related to the Police Chief. Doing that only encourages the speeding offender to continue to offend, and break traffic and speed rules. Lack of courage has consequences, and many-a-time those consequences are not desirable ones.

Now, I will introduce and discuss some of the livestock guardian breeds, who as per me, absolutely embody courage. Some of you may own these breeds, while some others may want to own them. I should mention that these breeds are typically not recommended for beginner pet owners, but their qualities do not preclude them from being pets in a family. One of the reasons for that advise is that these dogs have strong protective instincts, and they can sometimes be rather independent minded, which are not great qualities for novice pet dog owners.

Livestock Guardian Dog Breeds

As the name suggests, these breeds were bred for the purpose of protecting livestock from predators (usually wolves and bears). By dint of the purpose for which they were bred for, they had to be fearless and replete with fortitude. Take for instance, the Komondor (a beautiful dog originating from Hungary)—its name originates from its link with the Cuman people, who migrated from what is now present-day China to the Danube basin.[5,6] This dog has a lovely tasseled coat, which comes in handy when protecting herds of sheep. The coat provides both protection from the weather as well as from bites from predators. Additionally, the coat allows it to blend in with the Hungarian Racka Sheep.[7] They can literally act as a dog in a sheep's clothing, and thus lurk between the sheep. Woe betide any predator who thinks that the sheep are defenseless. One of my favorite sayings about the Komondor is that the dog will allow you to come into its backyard, but your leaving the backyard depends entirely on the dog.

While most of us will struggle to have a luxurious tasseled coat like the Komondor, we could certainly try and adopt some of its other qualities. As I mentioned earlier, the Komondor's tasseled coat allows it to blend in with the sheep it is protecting—that is such a neat concept for leaders to consider adopting. Essentially, if leaders get into the trenches to blend in (a little at least) with their followers, it'd make it much easier to not only lead but also to serve and protect followers. And, of course, having an indomitable sense of courage makes it a lot easier to play the role of protector.

Two other famous livestock guardian dog breeds, which originate from Türkiye are the Anatolian Shepherd and the Kangals. The AKC classifies

EMBODY THE BULLDOG SPIRIT/COURAGE 11

both breeds as being equivalent, but the UKC separates the two breeds, and in Türkiye too, the breeds are considered distinct from one another.[8] Regardless, they are both powerful and courageous dogs, who help protect their flocks from predators such as wolves (and sheep thieves as well). Indeed, the Anatolian Shepherd Dogs have been used in Namibia as well to help protect Cheetahs.[9,10] While it is amusing to imagine ranchers keeping corralled coalitions of cheetahs, which are all protected by their Anatolian Shepherd Dog protectors, the reality is a bit different. The dogs help protect cheetahs by deterring cheetahs from going after the flocks of livestock that they're guarding.

This then dissuades the ranchers from killing cheetahs. So, these dogs (both Anatolians and Kangals) have been used for multi-pronged protection purposes.

The parallel for humans is quite a straightforward one here. Unfortunately, we have many cases where leaders focus their attention on just one group of stakeholders (it usually tends to be the stockholders alone)—the Kangal example with the cheetah conservation project shows that a leader could benefit all by focusing on both direct and indirect stakeholders. Leaders who focus just on the bottom line should perhaps refocus their energy instead of focusing on the triple bottom line, which is sometimes termed as the three Ps (people, planet, and prosperity).[11,12]

Another dog breed that fits in with the discussion of courage is the Bouvier des Flanders.

This is a large Belgian breed, and its name roughly translates to Cowherd of Flanders. It is an iconic dog that has a very interesting story (even if apocryphal) associated with it. Apparently, the story goes, that a Bouvier des Flanders bit Adolf Hitler (in a rather sensitive area too). And then Hitler ordered his Nazi soldiers to kill every Bouvier des Flanders dog they came across, and that's why the breed was almost driven to extinction. While the story may be just a myth, you can see that the myth works just as well as reality would for one to discuss courage.

Sometimes courageous actions result in difficult and possibly devastating consequences, but leaders should still take those courageous actions. Regardless of the veracity of Hitler getting bitten by a Bouvier myth.[13,14] the fact of the matter is that Bouviers are very protective and courageous dogs. One could certainly pick up a modicum of courage from them.

And while we're on the topic of courage—it would be remiss of me to not mention the gentle giants from Switzerland, the Saint Bernard. The giant breed was bred by the monks of St. Bernard's Hospice in the Swiss Alps and is rather famously associated with being a courageous dog. These dogs were used in rescue operations, in order to find lost travelers. There is a rather apocryphal tale surrounding the dog as well. Essentially, while the part about them rescuing and comforting lost travelers in the mountainous Alps is accurate; it is not true that the Saint Bernard dogs had barrels of brandy sloshing in it, which was offered to the lost souls. While popular legend would have it that a warm swig of brandy would help warm up a frozen soul, the reality is that alcohol tends to dilate blood vessels, which in turn reduce overall core temperatures, which are not what frozen travelers need to have happen to them. In reality, the Saint Bernards were used to locate lost travelers, and sometimes revive them by warming them up by laying on top of them to provide them with much-needed heat.[15,16] One interesting historical fact about this breed is that the monks always name one of their Saint Bernards as Barry. This is an homage to a famous Saint Bernard named Barry (who lived from 1800 to 1814), who rescued more than 40 people, and famously rescued an unconscious lost boy who he first revived and then carried back to the monks. He did not proffer a swig of brandy to the rescued individuals as the apocryphal tale may suggest, but he did rescue several people.

Bully for Bulldogs

Now, let me talk about the raison d'etre of this chapter—the Bulldog. While there are many kinds of Bulldogs (including American Bulldogs, French Bulldogs, and Olde English Bulldogge), I am focusing my attention on the English Bulldog. Most people if asked about a Bulldog would automatically think of the English Bulldog, and that's why when I refer to the Bulldog, I will be referring to the English Bulldog. Any mention of the other Bulldog types will be depicted clearly.

The Bulldog's name comes from its original purpose, which was bullbaiting. That cruel sport involved dogs attacking bulls in the ring, during which the dogs would hang on to the bull's nose or throat. Resultantly, the dogs needed to have great grip power, and their wide heads and protruding lower jaws allowed them to breathe while holding on tight to the bull. This was all of course during the dark period when bullbaiting was a legal sport of sorts. The practice was outlawed in Britain in 1835,[2,3] but after that, breeders focused on reducing the aggression of the dog, and the Bulldog of yesteryear evolved into the good-natured companion dog we all know today. However, the qualities of the Bulldog including the courage aspect have continued to carry on forward.

England itself has adopted the Bulldog courage as a national symbol of courage.[17] While it originated during the nineteenth century, with political cartoonists using the Bulldog image juxtaposed with the female depiction of Britannia, I would state that the depiction became much firmer during the two World Wars. The Second World War (WWII) also had Winston Churchill in charge in England, who bore a striking physical resemblance to the Bulldog.

EMBODY THE BULLDOG SPIRIT/COURAGE

Therefore, the symbolism became even firmer. Of course, the present-day Bulldog stays far away from any bullpen, and is much more content to hang out in pristine living rooms; however, the legendary Bulldog courage has not ebbed away.

Another category of dogs that comes to mind when it comes to symbolizing courage are the breeds used chiefly by the military and law enforcement. This August list includes German Shepherds, Belgian Malinois, and Dutch Shepherds. Military, and law enforcement dogs have to practically demonstrate the greatest levels of courage, and that too, in circumstances that are filled to the brim with volatility and uncertainty. Let me discuss a bit about the German Shepherd. This is one of the most popular breeds out there, and an incredibly versatile one. My maternal grandparents had one (Ruby) and close friends of ours had another (Sherry). My wife also grew up with a whole squad of German Shepherds (they were all named Jimmy and Jikky). Apart from being used in the military and law enforcement context, they have been used in a variety of other contexts. Their original purpose was as a livestock guardian and herding dog; however, a German cavalry captain named Max von Stephanitz basically developed the breed, in the 1880s. The breed was registered in Germany in 1899, so essentially, the GSD (i.e., German Shepherd Dog) has been with us for almost 125 years now.[18,19] In this long-tenured run, the breed has become renowned for its versatility. GSDs are known for being highly trainable, and brave dogs.

And as I mentioned, Belgian Malinois and Dutch Shepherds too have become popular military and law enforcement dogs. One could perhaps argue that Belgian Malinois are now a lot more popular than the German Shepherds. A part of the reason is that the Belgian Malinois is a lighter dog, so it is easier for military personnel to be able to lift and carry the Belgian Malinois during military operations involving parachutes.[20] This particular breed originates from a Belgian city named Malines and has been used by the military since World War I.[21]

There was a Belgian Malinois named Cairo, who was with the Navy Seal team that tracked down Osama Bin Laden during that very dangerous mission. Another Belgian Malinois who became famous due to his bravery was a dog named Conan, who was injured in action while pursuing the ISIS leader Abu Bakr al-Baghdadi. Indeed, the US Navy Seals distinctly prefer Belgian Malinois, due to their better performance in skydiving. While the Belgian Malinois is the one that most people recognize, there are three other similar Belgian breeds called the Belgian Sheepdog, the Belgian Tervuren, and the Belgian Laekenois (all these dogs are basically distinguished by the color and type of their coats).[22]

14   LEARNING LEADERSHIP FROM DOGS

Dutch Shepherds are another breed, this time hailing from the Netherlands, as its name suggests. These dogs are smaller and lighter than both the German Shepherds and the Belgian Shepherds or Malinois, and have become very popular in law enforcement circles.[23] These brave dogs are used in both narcotics and bomb-disposal units in police work. They are also used as protection dogs. A friend of mine in the police department has exclusively worked with Dutch Shepherds and praises the gutsy determination of this breed. The popularity of the breed in law enforcement work is a little lower than the German Shepherds and Belgian Malinois, but regardless, is still a popular choice.

All of these dog breeds alluded to in this chapter provide immensely valuable services for humans. As I mentioned previously, farmers and livestock breeders owe a lot to their livestock guardians. Similarly, police officers and military personnel owe their very lives to their canine companions. A friend of mine was a bomb disposal unit soldier in the US Army, and the bond he shared with his military dog was unbreakable. The dog literally saved his life and many of his colleagues' lives on many occasions, and I have no doubt that any military or law enforcement personnel in similar roles would echo the same sentiment.

Being Bravehearts

The courage that these various breeds of dogs display is something that should provide us humans food for thought. Many of us give up in the face of danger or risk, just because we are usually risk averse. Being courageous does not of course equate to being reckless or stupid—however, if there is a slight chance of success, then it does behoove us to take that chance. As individuals, we often have a choice when making decisions on various matters, be they personal or professional in nature. These choices often determine whether or not we are fully utilizing our courage, or if we are simply choosing the easiest and least-anxiety-provoking option.

Sometimes, duties and responsibilities are unpleasant in nature, and require sacrifices to be made. Consider the case of a leader who has to choose between an incredibly unpopular decision, but an important one for the financial solvency of the company, or a non-decision which would simply push the eventual insolvency to a different time. The courageous choice would be to carry out the unpopular decision, and not just to kick the can down the road. A CEO (now retired) told me once that if he ever had to lay a lot of people off or close a facility, then he would make sure to go there in person and do so himself. He said he found it appalling when leaders would outsource such unpleasant duties to others, in order to avoid discomfort. Very cowardly of a leader to do that.

EMBODY THE BULLDOG SPIRIT/COURAGE   15

Besides the big decisions that require courage, there are smaller decisions too that require a modicum of courage to handle. Think about one of the biggest charges of leadership—yes, I refer to the process of delegation. Woe betide any company that is afflicted with a myopic micromanaging leader in charge. That sort of leader is afraid, nay, petrified of allowing his or her followers any duties or responsibilities, which they have the freedom to decide on. Instead, the micromanager ends up doing and dictating everything that everyone in the company does. The element of freedom is absolutely nonexistent, and one can trace micromanagement with a distinct lack of courage. When one lacks the courage to even allow a follower to fail, then one is giving up any chance of that follower growing and succeeding on his or her own merits. I do exhort you, gentle reader, to avoid with as much firmness as you can, the tendency to micromanage. Practice the judicious art of empowered delegation[24,25]—a leader doing everything for the entire team or organization is a sheer waste of effort and suboptimal use of talent. Instead, use a bit of courage to start taking decisions that may seem risky for you, but unless you take a bit of risk, you are never going to achieve the best potential outcome.

Honestly, while it can seem intimidating to be courageous, especially in situations of strife and discomfort, the alternative options are never quite worth the temporary comfort. Take a bone from any of the many courageous dog breeds out there—if those dogs can display extreme displays of courage in the most dangerous circumstances, then why can't we emulate that? Most individuals will not even be in similarly dangerous situations (unless of course, one is in a dangerous occupation), so it's not asking for too much to expect a little bit of courage. The courage to do the right thing and the courage to take on and tackle discomfort is something we can all do. Leaders have the responsibility (even if not explicitly spelled out) of protecting their companies and followers. They can accomplish these tasks a lot more efficiently simply by embodying courage, especially the kind of courage that dog breeds like the many discussed in this chapter exemplify. The next chapter will focus on communication, and I will discuss the importance of communication for leaders.

Summary

This chapter discussed courage, and I described and discussed several dog breeds who are renowned across the world for their courage and determination. I trust the reader will have a bit more understanding of these various dogs, as well as internalize the importance of courage, in a leadership context. Next, let me communicate to you the importance of communication, be it verbal or nonverbal. Or rather, I will be doing that in chapter three.

16 LEARNING LEADERSHIP FROM DOGS

Anatolian Shepherd Dog   Komondor

Kangal   Bouvier des Flanders

St. Bernard   Belgian Malinois

German Shepherd   Bulldog

Belgian Sheepdog

Belgian Tervuren

Belgian Laekenois

Dutch Shepherd

References

1 https://barkvoiceofthebulldogs.org/946/features/the-history-of-bulldogs/.
2 https://www.akc.org/expert-advice/lifestyle/9-things-you-didnt-know-about-the-bulldog/.
3 https://doglawreporter.blogspot.com/2012/06/sordid-history-of-pit-bull-fighting-in.html.
4 Pedersen, N. C., Pooch, A. S., & Liu, H. (2016). A genetic assessment of the English bulldog. *Canine Genetics and Epidemiology*, 3, 1–16.
5 Kincses-Nagy, É. (2013). A disappeared people and a disappeared language the Cumans and the Cuman language in Hungary. *Tehlikedeki Diller Dergisi*, 2(2), 171–186.
6 https://www.akc.org/expert-advice/dog-breeds/komondor-history-behind-the-breed/.
7 http://rackasheep.com/the-breed/.
8 https://fotp.com/learn/dog-lifestyle/know-your-dog-breeds-anatolian-shepherd-vs-kangal.
9 https://www.dailysabah.com/turkey/2017/02/09/kangal-vs-cheetah-turkish-lion-protects-namibias-herds.
10 https://cheetah.org/canada/about-us/what-we-support/livestock-guarding-dogs-program/.
11 Norman, W., & MacDonald, C. (2004). Getting to the bottom of "triple bottom line". *Business Ethics Quarterly*, 14(2), 243–262.

LEARNING LEADERSHIP FROM DOGS

12 Willard, B. (2012). *The New Sustainability Advantage: Seven Business Case Benefits of a Triple Bottom Line.* New Society Publishers: Gabriola Island, Canada.

13 https://www.akc.org/expert-advice/dog-breeds/bouvier-des-flandres-history-belgiums-farm-dog-germanys-enemy/.

14 https://nationalpurebreddogday.com/the-reason-for-evils-monorchism/.

15 https://www.akc.org/dog-breeds/st-bernard/.

16 https://www.thedailybeast.com/the-myth-of-the-st-bernard-and-the-brandy-barrel.

17 https://greatbritishmag.co.uk/uk-culture/why-is-the-bulldog-a-symbol-of-britain/.

18 https://www.akc.org/dog-breeds/german-shepherd-dog/.

19 https://www.thekennelclub.org.uk/search/breeds-a-to-z/breeds/pastoral/german-shepherd-dog/.

20 https://www.defense.gov/Multimedia/Experience/Four-Legged-Fighters/#:~:text=The%20only%20breed%20the%20program,Shepherds%20but%20are%20more%20compact.

21 https://www.akc.org/dog-breeds/belgian-malinois/.

22 https://www.akc.org/dog-breeds/belgian-tervuren/.

23 https://www.akc.org/dog-breeds/dutch-shepherd/.

24 McConnell, C. R. (1995). Delegation versus empowerment: What, how, and is there a difference? *The Health Care Manager,* 14(1), 69–79.

25 Lee, M., & Koh, J. (2001). Is empowerment really a new concept? *International Journal of Human Resource Management,* 12(4), 684–695.

Chapter 3

(COLLIE)TY COMMUNICATION

Communication and Its Various Forms

There are several kinds of communication that one could discuss in this chapter, and I will do so at length in this chapter. On the one hand, we have the nonverbal variety, where one understands the message being conveyed even without any sound. The other kind of communication is obviously of the spoken variety, where language and sound play their respective parts. Then there is the written aspect of communication, which is what is being used here in this book, after all (at least until the imminently inevitable audiobook, when the medium of communication would shift to the spoken kind of communication. David Tennant would make an excellent narrator, I think, but I digress. Back to the chapter!).

As always, a definition of communication would be helpful before we get deeper into the topic itself. Communication involved the transmission and reception of information, and that information can be received or relayed via different means, be it oral, nonverbal, or written. If there is information that needs to be shared with others, then communication is the way to go about doing so. Now since this book is about how we can learn and improve our own leadership from dogs, I am not going to focus too much on the written form of communication. Sadly, dogs are yet to master the art of writing—there are no canine equivalents of William Shakespeare or J. K. Rowling. Yes, dogs are amazing in the art of listening (well, some dogs are experts in selective listening, like mine when she doesn't want to go back home from the dog park), and that is a huge part of communication too. But as far as the written aspect of communication is concerned, dogs are sadly a nonstarter there. So, let's begin with the nonverbal aspect of communication, which one must admit, dogs are experts in both relaying as well as understanding.[1-3]

Nonverbal Communication

This form of communication is perhaps one that dogs are masterful practitioners of; many a dog can simply stare into their human's eyes and let them know exactly what the dog is conveying. My dogs for one have always demonstrated the unflinching ability to gaze into my eyes and convey exactly what it is that they wish. It's uncanny, and usually always accurate. I am not as good at understanding what some humans are conveying in a nonverbal way; sometimes of course, but not always. But dogs are a different animal entirely, no pun intended. Dogs can communicate in a variety of nonverbal ways, and some of those ways offer some neat lessons for us noncanids. I will now discuss some dog breeds that are experts in nonverbal communication.

This naturally points us toward Pointers, Setters, and Spaniels (to a lesser degree). These dogs are categorized as gundogs because they are associated with hunters, usually birds and small game hunters. This category also includes Retrievers, but for the purposes of nonverbal communication, they don't really work as an example. The Pointers as their name signifies point toward the location of the prey. They basically freeze into position, with their nose, body, and tail all in alignment. Essentially, they stand still, with a foot raised and their nose pointing in the direction of the game. There is no sound involved here—silent posing which clearly indicates to the hunter where the game is to be found.

There are several kinds of Pointers—the English Pointer, the German Shorthaired Pointer, the German Wirehaired Pointer, the German Longhaired Pointer, and the Wirehaired Pointing Griffon, and many rarer Pointers such as the French Gascony Pointer, the Spanish Pointer, the Danish Pointer, and the French Pyrenean Pointer. All of these dogs have been around since the 1700s, and so have a rich history of being represented in art and literature (such as Ponto from Charles Dickens' *The Pickwick Papers*).[4–6] The English Pointer may have been around as early as the 1650s. In the very beginning, they were used to point hare for the larger Greyhounds to pursue; however, since the eighteenth century, after shooting birds on the wing became popular with hunters, the Pointer started to directly point at the hunter.

The German Pointers come in a variety of coats—the short-haired variety, the long-haired variety, and the wire-haired variety.[5] These dogs have very similar temperaments, and all point in similar ways. The same can be said to be true of the other rarer Pointers, but they all point in the same way, and all in a rather non-verbal way. In a way, one could pretty much liken this behavior to path–goal leadership.[7] Leaders too often have to act as Pointers of a sort—they point their employees and followers to the main goal.

Another gundog breed that is particularly applicable to be discussed here is the Setter group. There are primarily four types of Setters—English Setters, Irish Setters, Irish Red and White Setters, Gordon Setters, and Llewellyn Setters.[8–12] These dogs are beautiful gun dogs, and their name arises from their particular nonverbal behavior. They "set" down when they encounter prey— what it means to "set" is basically to crouch motionlessly to hint to the human

(COLLIE)TY COMMUNICATION

hunters, that the prey is near. This is beautiful nonverbal communication because just like their Pointer cousins, the Setters are basically leading their hunters to the main goal.

I will briefly discuss each of the Setter types here. From my vantage point, I am rather partial to the Gordon Setter (the most handsome of all Setters, but that's not to say that the other Setters are mere slouches in the looks department). They are all beautiful and even-tempered dogs. The Gordon Setter is a black and tan dog, which has the characteristic feathered tail that is common to all Setters. As its name suggests, the breed was helped in its journey of legitimacy by kennel clubs, thanks to the Duke of Gordon (Alexander Gordon), who established a Gordon Setter kennel at Castle Gordon in Scotland.[9] Essentially, the good Duke did not invent the breed, but he helped give it legitimacy, and of course, gave it the Gordon name. The Gordon Setter tends to be the heaviest and largest kind of Setter.

The English Setter on the other hand tends to have the most dramatically different coat colors. Sometimes, they are blue, lemon, orange, chestnut Belton, or roan. Edward Laverack is the person credited with creating the specific line of Setters that are known to us today.[13] Just like their Gordon cousins, the English Setter too is a gentle and good-natured breed. This breed also displays the nonverbal behavior of "setting" in order to alert the hunter to the presence of prey. Ditto with the Irish Setter and the Irish Red and White Setter—the Irish Setter is a handsome Red or Mahogany coat-colored dog, and similarly good-natured as its other Setter cousins. The Red and White Setter, as its name suggests, has a red and white coat. I've known friends who have had working Setters, and they were remarkable in their temperaments and their nonverbal communication skills.

Both Pointers and Setters' behaviors can be clearly tied in with how good and effective leaders operate. Leaders may not need to physically point or crouch down on their haunches like Pointers and Setters, but showcasing a path forward is definitely good form for any leader. Leaders obviously should expect results from their followers; however, it also behooves them to help their followers in achieving those good results. One of the worst kinds of leaders out there is the lackadaisical or laissez-faire leader.[14,15] That category of leader does nothing, says nothing, and helps with nothing. They leave you alone to swim or sink, as the case may be. Yes, they don't harass you like micromanagers do, but then again, if they don't contribute at all, what exactly is the point of them being leaders. One may as well just not have any leader then, right? I would rather be a leader who points the way to my followers than be a laissez-faire leader who does nothing of the sort. This particular category of leadership has been found by several scholars as being linked with the least amount of productivity in followers as well as other negative outcomes.[14–17]

22 LEARNING LEADERSHIP FROM DOGS

While the "pointing" and "setting" are quite distinctly nonverbal behaviors by specific breeds of dogs, there are other nonverbal behaviors that are somewhat common to a variety of dog breeds. A lot of dogs extensively communicate with nonverbal cues and behaviors, such as tail wags, ear wiggles, paw pokes, soul-searching stares, and so on. There are also some breeds that don't bark, and are considered "quiet." The Basenji is one such dog breed—it's a dog that hails from Central Africa, specifically Congo.[18] The Basenji does not bark, instead it yodels. That is due to the shape of its larynx, which differs from other dog breeds. The Basenji is also known as a Schensi dog or the Congo Terrier or the Bush Dog. However, the Basenji appears to be the name that it is most known for. Traditional pygmy hunters used Basenjis to drive big game into nets, and the way by which they would do so was by having bells hung around their necks to scare the prey into the nets.[19] A mouse may struggle to bell a cat, but pygmy hunters did not seem to have any trouble in belling their Basenjis.

Another dog breed that comes to mind when it comes to striking nonverbal behavior is the ever-smiling Samoyed. This dog breed was developed by the nomadic Samoyedic people of Siberia.[20] As its name and origin suggest, this dog comes equipped with a heavy warm coat. Indeed, present-day Samoyed owners often state that their Samoyeds often cuddle up with their owners and family members when it's cooler weather. This particular nonverbal behavior comes embedded in them thanks to their ancient origins, where they would be used as hot-water bottles of a sort to warm up children and their owners during the bitter-cold Siberian winters.[21] If one employs a metaphor for this, it is very similar to a leader having to warm up their followers during a bitter winter. Not literally of course, but still, when times are tough, leaders should consider borrowing a leaf from Samoyeds and assist with keeping their followers warm and safe from frostbite.

Another great example of nonverbal behavior displayed by dogs is the behavior displayed by Australian Cattle Dogs. These dogs are also called Blue Heelers and sometimes Red Heelers, and as their name suggests are from Australia (specifically Queensland is sometimes part of their name). English settlers brought dogs to Australia and bred them with Dingoes, and this eventually led to the creation of Australian Cattle Dogs.[22,23] This energetic breed gets its name from its penchant for nipping at the heels of cattle in order to get them to go a certain direction or to herd them a certain way. In many ways, this can be similar to a leader urging their followers to adhere to a certain plan or to follow a certain course of action. The trouble arises when the followers don't exactly appreciate the "nipping" behavior. That's where a certain level of Follower–Leader fit certainly helps; but one must remember that this sort of leader "nipping" behavior is eons better than the lackadaisical nonbehaviors exhibited by laissez-faire leaders.

(COLLIE)TY COMMUNICATION

Next, I will discuss the verbal behaviors that dogs demonstrate, and relate them back to lessons that leaders can learn.

Why Won't You Listen to Me?

Dogs have differing ways of barking. As I mentioned earlier, some breeds like Basenjis don't even bark. Some others howl (most Hounds), and some sing. I refer here to the New Guinea Singing Dog. That dog has the amazing ability of being able to change the notes of its howling, which makes it sound like it is singing. Try listening to a "song session" on YouTube by a New Guinea Singing Dog. It sounds pretty good. The dog however is still sort of feral and only semidomesticated.[24] So unfortunately, I do not have a whole lot of discussion to make about that particular breed. After this awkward juncture, let us press on to a different breed, one that is most definitely not feral.

Border Collies are one of the most recognizable and intelligent dogs out there, and what beautiful workers they are. Border Collies typically work silently, but every now and again, they have to bark at their charges to get them to move in a certain direction. As their name suggests, Border Collies originated at the border, specifically between England and Scotland.[25] They generally work silently by gazing at their herd and getting them to comply. However, there are indubitably times when a gaze alone doesn't work; in those cases, a sharp bark can often do the trick better. Leaders can take a trick from this too—sometimes, their tried and tested methods may simply not work. In those cases, they may have to adapt their style a bit—indeed, the silent types of leaders may need to start getting garrulous, while the voluble sorts of leaders may need to start getting a trifle bit taciturn. Adaptive leadership is where it's at! The ability to be able to adapt your leadership style so that it best fits a given situation is a very important ability for leaders to possess.

I know of leaders who are experts in using adaptive leadership. They are directive with individuals who prefer a directive approach, and they are more hands-off with individuals who prefer to be more empowered. Following an opposite style with individuals could seriously backfire. In many of my graduate course discussions on leadership and organizational behavior, I have often been left bewildered by some of the horror stories I've heard about errant leaders. A lot of those horror stories seem to feature leaders who follow opposite styles of leading with people who prefer something else. In a way, it would be like expecting an Italian Greyhound to go galloping along the frozen Tundra like an Alaskan Malamute—it simply isn't effective, is it?

Therefore, I believe that effective communication needs to be tailored to the intended recipients' preferences. If your recipient likes getting his or her information delivered in a face-to-face one-on-one setting, then it behooves

24 LEARNING LEADERSHIP FROM DOGS

you to try to do that. If you can't do it for any reason, at least try to approximate the delivery. Perhaps, an intimate WebEX or Zoom session would work as well? Do not send an impersonal stack of documents to that person who expects communication to be personal. Alternately, of course, do not force one-on-one meetings with individuals, who prefer getting information through formal or written documentation. There is no need for you to force that individual into a one-on-one meeting, is there? It may be your personal style of communication, but you have to tailor it to your recipient, in order for that communication to be effective.

Back to the listening component of communication—imagine trying to communicate with someone, and they're not listening to you but instead trying to get you to listen to them. in that sort of situation, there will be exactly zero information transmitted. For clarity of communication, one party must listen. As far as listening is concerned, there are a few dog breeds out there that are champions of listening. These breeds are renowned for their skills in obedience. Let me talk about the Standard Poodle here. A lot of people want the Poodle characteristics, but with an exotic flair about it, and hence go in for the variety of Doodles out there. It is of course entirely a different matter that all the qualities they're looking for in Doodles come from the Poodle, so they may as well get a Poodle. Anyway, setting that bit of logic aside, let us dive a bit into the world of Poodles.

Most people associate Poodles with France, and indeed, France proudly claims the Poodle for itself. However, it is likely that Poodles actually originated from Germany.[26] Even the name is based on the word *Pudelin* which means to splash in water. The Poodle is one of the most trainable and obedient dogs out there—the amount of agility tricks that Poodles can do is simply splendid. Poodles were retrieving water dogs in the beginning, however, over time they have become ubiquitous with agility and have also achieved a large level of fame in the circus and carnival circuit. Poodles are the perfect breed to showcase communication because they are a breed of dog that have shown time and again excellent capacity to understand and comprehend about 400 different words. This is about twice as many words as other dogs are usually able to understand. As one can gather, the more words someone understands, the better it is to be able to communicate with them.

Feedback Is Important for Communication

While most of what I've talked about in the preceding sections involves around communication, it would be remiss of me to not even mention feedback. Too often, leaders and non-leaders alike fall into the trap of communicating without building into a component of feedback. Imagine that you are at a

(COLLIE)TY COMMUNICATION

restaurant and you order half-a-dozen tacos. The chef dutifully makes the first three, and you start eating those, only to discover that the spice level on them is rather too much for you. If at this stage, you don't provide any feedback to the chef, then you will be left with having to eat six fiery tacos or risk insulting the chef by not eating all of the food on your plate. Neither option is optimal, and in fact, they are both instances of a no-feedback component. If the chef had canvassed feedback early on, then the spice could have been adjusted to suit the customer better. And conversely, if the customer had indicated their discomfort with the spice level by providing early feedback, then the situation could have been salvaged by the chef. Without feedback, the final outcome is tragically suboptimal. A leader who does not provide feedback or who does not canvas feedback is going to have suboptimal communication through and through. The feedback loop needs to be present throughout the communication process, in order for the communication to be effective.

When it comes to dogs, one typically sees feedback being used in the context of training. Especially, in terms of positive and negative reinforcement, being used as tools of feedback. Positive reinforcement usually involves treats and praise, while negative reinforcement involves scolding. As one could guess, positive reinforcement generally works a lot better than negative reinforcement. One of the dog breeds that tends to be super receptive to positive reinforcement is the sprightly Beagle. Most people would be familiar with Beagles, thanks to the ubiquitous presence of Snoopy, who is possibly the most famous Beagle in comics, thanks to Peanuts. The Beagle itself is one of the most popular hound breeds in the US and regularly makes it into the top ten breeds by popularity.[27]

Dog historians believe that while early ancestors of Beagles were around in England much before the arrival of the Roman legions in Britain. However, the modern Beagle most likely traces its origins to the now-extinct Talbot Hound (which was the ancestor of both the Beagle as well as the Bloodhound).[28] Beagles tend to be extraordinarily food motivated, and as a result, are particularly amenable to positive reinforcement. One of the famous Beagles in recent times is Roscoe, who happens to be a specialist in sniffing out bedbugs (those creepy bugs have resurged like nobody's business in the past two decades). Additionally, Beagles are fantastic at sniffing out food; as a result, the US Department of Agriculture started a Beagle Brigade back in 1984, which has Beagles helping sniff out illegal foods at various border crossings. While it may seem like a bit too much to seize people's "illegal" foods, the possible negative consequences to US agriculture mandate the necessity of a Beagle Brigade.

So back to feedback, leaders must ensure that they allow for their followers to deliver and receive feedback. It is important to always follow up with each other to ensure that actual communication occurs. There is no point in communicating if neither the sender nor the receiver is even aware of whether or not the actual message is going through. While communication is certainly important, and both verbal and nonverbal communication equally so, without a feedback component, it is likely to be useless in information relaying and gathering. Therefore, leaders should not only focus on delivering and listening to good communication, they should focus on ensuring that a constant feedback loop is prevalent in their communication. Chapter 4 will focus on authenticity, and I will discuss the importance of being authentic leaders.

Summary

In this chapter, I discussed and focused on the importance of communication, both verbal as well as nonverbal. I also described several breeds of dogs, who are especially pertinent in discussions revolving around communication. I also emphasize in this chapter how feedback is essential in ensuring the validity of communication. In Chapter 4, I will be talking about authenticity, and how important it is for leaders to be authentic leaders.

Pointer   German Pointer

Irish Setter   Gordon Setter

(COLLIE)TY COMMUNICATION

Basenji

Australian Cattle Dog

Samoyed

New Guinea Singing Dog

Beagle

Poodle

Border Collie

English Setter

References

1 Meyer, I., & Forkman, B. (2014). Nonverbal communication and human–dog interaction. *Anthrozoös*, 27(4), 553–568.
2 Walsh, E. A., Meers, L. L., Samuels, W. E., Boonen, D., Claus, A., Duarte-Gan, C., ... & Normando, S. (2024). Human-dog communication: How body language and non-verbal cues are key to clarity in dog directed play, petting and hugging behaviour by humans. *Applied Animal Behaviour Science*, 272, 106206.
3 Kaminski, J., & Nitzschner, M. (2013). Do dogs get the point? A review of dog–human communication ability. *Learning and Motivation*, 44(4), 294–302.
4 https://www.akc.org/dog-breeds/pointer/.
5 https://www.akc.org/dog-breeds/german-shorthaired-pointer/.
6 https://victorianweb.org/art/illustration/seymour/3.html.
7 House, R. J. (1971). A path goal theory of leader effectiveness. *Administrative Science Quarterly*, 16(3), 321–339.
8 https://www.akc.org/dog-breeds/english-setter/.
9 https://www.thekennelclub.org.uk/search/breeds-a-to-z/breeds/gundog/gordon-setter/.
10 https://www.akc.org/dog-breeds/irish-setter/.
11 https://ckcusa.com/breeds/llewellin-setter/.
12 https://www.akc.org/expert-advice/dog-breeds/irish-red-and-white-setter-history/.
13 https://www.thekennelclub.org.uk/search/breeds-a-to-z/breeds/gundog/english-setter/.
14 Skogstad, A., Einarsen, S., Torsheim, T., Aasland, M. S., & Hetland, H. (2007). The destructiveness of laissez-faire leadership behavior. *Journal of Occupational Health Psychology*, 12(1), 80–92.
15 Buch, R., Martinsen, Ø. L., & Kuvaas, B. (2015). The destructiveness of laissez-faire leadership behavior: The mediating role of economic leader–member exchange relationships. *Journal of Leadership & Organizational Studies*, 22(1), 115–124.
16 Hinkin, T. R., & Schriesheim, C. A. (2008). An examination of "nonleadership": From laissez-faire leadership to leader reward omission and punishment omission. *Journal of Applied Psychology*, 93(6), 1234–1248.
17 Breevaart, K., & Zacher, H. (2019). Main and interactive effects of weekly transformational and laissez-faire leadership on followers' trust in the leader and leader effectiveness. *Journal of Occupational and Organizational Psychology*, 92(2), 384–409.
18 https://www.akc.org/dog-breeds/basenji/.
19 http://www.basenji-freunde.com/pygmies.htm.
20 https://www.akc.org/dog-breeds/samoyed/.
21 http://www.nswsamoyedclub.com/about-the-breed.html.
22 https://www.akc.org/dog-breeds/australian-cattle-dog/.
23 https://www.thekennelclub.org.uk/search/breeds-a-to-z/breeds/pastoral/australian-cattle-dog/.
24 https://ckcusa.com/breeds/new-guinea-singing-dog/.
25 https://www.thekennelclub.org.uk/search/breeds-a-to-z/breeds/pastoral/border-collie/.
26 https://www.thekennelclub.org.uk/search/breeds-a-to-z/breeds/utility/poodle-standard/.
27 https://www.akc.org/dog-breeds/beagle/.
28 https://www.akc.org/expert-advice/dog-breeds/beagle-history/#:~:text=Modern%2Dday%20Beagles%20are%20thought,tan%20dogs%20similar%20to%20Bloodhounds.

Chapter 4

OTTERLY (O)AUTHENTICITY

Authenticity in Individuals

I have always felt that authenticity is a quality that should be encouraged in leaders, and non-leaders alike. After all, why waste time and effort being an individual who is faker than a shiny glistening snowball in the middle of the Sahara Desert. There is nothing quite as unmotivating as finding out that a person especially someone in a position of authority to you (such as your leader) is inauthentic, and that their words mean nothing and have no value whatsoever. Authenticity refers to the quality of being genuine—in other words, you speak in accordance with what you actually believe or think. If you adhere to a certain value-system, then you act in accordance with it.[1,2] For example, if you profess to be a vegan, but find yourself sneaking off to the local churrascaria every weekend to binge on picanha; then it is apparent that you are not authentically vegan. A lack of genuineness reflects a lack of authenticity, and of course, leaders who are not authentic cannot be said to be authentic leaders.

In this chapter, I will be focusing on authenticity and more precisely authentic leadership. While a person can be authentic without being a leader, an authentic leader cannot be one without being authentic. Authentic leadership is one of the more recent theories out there in the discipline of leadership and has certainly captivated the attention of scholars and popular-press people alike. As I said, we all love the very concept of authenticity—we want the items we purchase to be genuine, and we want the people we associate with to be genuine as well. That sentiment is amplified when it comes to leaders—followers crave for their leaders to be authentic leaders, as it's a lot easier for someone to follow an authentic leader.

Now back to our canine companions—I have personally never met a single dog who has been less than authentic. Yes, some are mischievous, and many are quirky characters, but they are always authentic. The love and adoration they bestow on their loved ones is always enveloped with 100% FDA-approved authenticity. If you consider some of the theoretical backgrounds of authentic leadership theory, you'll find that one oft-used system breaks down authentic leadership into four components, namely self-awareness, balanced

30 LEARNING LEADERSHIP FROM DOGS

processing, moral perspective, and relational transparency.[3] I am going to dive a bit deeper into these four areas and discuss examples of how certain dog breeds really fit the bill, in terms of authentic leadership. I am going to start off with self-awareness first!

Self-Awareness and Dogs

You may have all seen the widely reported headline that some dogs are self-aware, even though they don't pass the mirror test.[4–6] That particular headline was generated due to an article, which found that dogs had body awareness and were able to control the movements of their bodies in experimental conditions where they had to do so in order to grab a toy. This led the science experimentalists to propose that even if dogs fail the mirror test, they do at least show some level of self-awareness. However, the self-awareness that I'll be talking about vis-à-vis authentic leadership is a trifle bit different. This component of authentic leadership has to do with how individuals understand themselves and know their own strengths and weaknesses. Dogs typically know their own strengths and weaknesses, although to be fair, this is not wholly applicable across the entire canine kingdom. Some dogs do exist who seem to not know their own strengths or weaknesses and pick on fights that they cannot possibly win or engage in stunts which are impossible to pull off. But on the whole, barring the canine individuals who are Daredevils without a cause, most dogs seem to be keenly aware of what they can and what they cannot do.

Herding breeds (such as the previously discussed Border Collies, for instance) know that they are excellent at herding animals. Many a family has noticed that their pet herding breed dog will often attempt to herd their other pets and their children, and sometimes even the actual adults in the family. This is because herding breeds know that they are great at herding others (that does not work too well with cats, but that's a topic for a different day and a different book). Ditto with French Bulldogs—they seem to know that they're not really designed for the water, but there's always the rare individual French Bulldog who fancies he or she is a Labrador Retriever. For anyone reading this who is contemplating getting a French Bulldog, please make sure to supervise your Frenchie and not leave them hanging out in the pool by themselves, just in case, your particular dog happens to be a rare Daredevil, who is unaware of their own strengths and weaknesses.

I suppose the above paragraph compels one to jot down a bit more about the French Bulldog.[7,8] This particular breed is essentially descended from English Toy Bulldogs, which were taken to France back in the nineteenth century. The distinctive difference between Frenchies and their more rotund English cousins is the erect Bat Ears of French Bulldogs. A historical fact which will interest readers is that in the beginning, Frenchies were very popular with the proprietors and staff of Parisian brothels. As many humorous titles proclaim, Frenchies went from being popular in brothels to being popular with lace makers and finally with royals![9] The breed was intended to be a companion dog, and it is an amazing companion dog. A happy and giving and craving love kind of dog. However, as I mentioned earlier, they cannot swim! For them is not the destiny of the salty sea, unless they are equipped with lifejackets. This inability to swim is because of the way they're bred and designed—French Bulldogs tend to be pretty top-heavy, and as a result, tend to sink rather than float. It also does not help that they have big heads compared with their bodies, which accentuates the whole top-heavy nature of their bodies.

Dogs that are equipped with webbed feet and are specifically bred for retrieving purposes, on the other hand, know that they can swim, and nobody has to really train them in that aspect. It comes naturally to all Retriever types, be it Chesapeake Bay Retrievers, Labrador Retrievers, Golden Retrievers, Flat-Coated Retrievers, and so on. So, one could easily claim that most Retrievers are rather high on self-awareness. Now is as good a time as any to discuss the Labrador Retriever, which is one of the best and most popular family pets across the globe.[10,11] This particular breed is easily recognizable and comes in a variety of colors, such as yellow, chocolate, and black. The Labrador Retriever did not originate in Labrador, but instead had its ancestors in Newfoundland. The original ancestor was the St. John's Water Dog (a now-extinct breed), but which had both Newfoundlands and Labrador Retrievers descend from it. Labradors and their close cousins, the Golden Retrievers, are both the finest dogs to be used as seeing-eye dogs for the visually impaired. Their self-awareness is simply brilliant to notice, and they are equally versatile as tracking dogs for law enforcement. From a people perspective, I guess, one of the lessons is to know thyself. Like a Frenchie or a Labrador knows their own swimming skills, a human individual must learn about his or her own personal strengths and weaknesses. Unless one spends a bit of time in reflection, one cannot begin to truly know oneself, and gaining an appreciation for and awareness of oneself, is truly the first step toward becoming more of an authentic leader yourself.

Next, I'm going to segue into balanced processing and discuss how certain dog breeds exemplify that aspect of authentic leadership.

Balanced Processing and Dogs

Now on the surface of it, balanced processing basically refers to self-regulation,[3] and more specifically, refers to being able to take into consideration outside feedback. For me, there is no other breed that best exemplifies this quality than the sublimely spectacular Rough Collie. When I was growing up, I was an avid reader of Enid Blyton books, and one of my all-time favorite books of all was *Shadow, the Sheep-Dog*. It's about a Collie named Shadow, who lives as a working dog/pet on a farm. I recently bought the book (it's sadly out of print now, so you can only purchase used copies of it), and my kids loved it. Absolutely loved it! The book is a spectacular read, and you actually learn quite a bit about Collies, and how they work together in cohesion on the farm, while doing their primary job of shepherding.

And of course, if you haven't read the book (no surprise, it is sadly out of print now), you would have at least heard about the Lassie movie series, which features the titular Collie who does a lot for her family (it is a slightly amusing fact that all of the canine actors in the Lassie series were male dogs). So back to Collies—there is another type of Collie called the Smooth Collie, which is essentially a milder, calmer, and short-coated version of the Rough Collie. The Smooth Collie is a wonderful breed, which has had great success being used as a guide dog for patients suffering from Alzheimer's disease.[12] Queen Victoria was perhaps the biggest proponent of both these breeds and kept many dogs of both breeds in her kennels. The Collie is today perhaps used more as a pet dog and has been replaced largely by the Border Collie, as a serious shepherd dog in the UK, but the Rough Collie is increasingly seeing an uptick in popularity as a working dog in the US.[13,14]

The Rough Collie though is the more popular among the duo, in terms of numbers and visual recognition. More people would recognize a Rough Collie than they would a Smooth Collie, just because the Rough Collie has had a ton more media exposure than the Smooth Collie has. So, in terms of balanced processing, what the Rough Collie does on the shepherding front is rather a marvel to witness. They have to obviously consider the commands of the human shepherd (who may be rough in appearance human but a smooth soul on the whole), but they also have to balance that information out with other information that they obtain from their fellow sheepdogs, and even from the sheep themselves. The original command may have been to take a flock of sheep all the way to a particular field, but perhaps, there is an obstruction or impediment at that destination—in that case, the Collies have to consider that new information and change the overall processing of it in real time.

Humans could learn a lot from our Collie counterparts—imagine being able to not only process real-time information but also be able to balance it with prior information. Think about the people who rigidly adhere to archaic stodgy rules, just because those rules have existed for a while. Such individuals are not following balanced processing at all—indeed, balanced processing means that they should consider new information and take that into account while possibly modifying their earlier actions or actions in progress. So, in other words, take the time to shed your rigidity somewhat

OTTERLY (O)AUTHENTICITY

and be a bit more flexible, in listening to other people's perspectives, and also consider changing circumstances and situations. Blindly charging ahead with an older plan, which no longer fits current circumstances, would be foolish in the extreme. Balanced processing is a very important aspect of being able to embody authentic leadership—it all boils down to shedding your rigidity, and embracing the fluidity of new data and new occurrences. In simpler terms, we need to work on improving our responses in the face of change—as the old chestnut aphorism says, change is constant, and we must constantly change in response to it. Only then can we hope to improve our balanced processing – we sure can learn a lot about that from Collies. Now, I will transition along to the moral perspective, which is the third component of authentic leadership.

Moral Perspective and Dogs

Now readers may think that this particular dimension can be a bit of a puzzle, especially in terms of how exactly moral perspective applies to dogs. Can dogs (regardless of breed) truly possess a moral perspective on matters? To gauge that, all you have to think about is the variety of news articles out there that allude to the protective actions that dogs have taken throughout history. Saving a child from a burning building? Dogs have done that.

Protecting a family member from an external threat? Dogs have done that too. There are thousands of TikTok and Instagram videos that show that many dogs truly possess a good perspective on fairness and doing the right thing. Equity theory (where an individual compares his or her rewards with another to gauge whether or not the reward is fair compared with the effort) is a theory that works astoundingly well on dogs.[15,16] If a dog notices that another dog is getting better rewards for doing similar work, that dog is quite likely to bark up or restrict its own performance due to the injustice of it all.

For me, a breed that really exemplifies this quality of internalized moral perspective is the Otterhound.[17] I may be super biased about this, especially since I have an Otterhound myself. Fiona is the most darling Otterhound out there in a sadly dwindling pond of Otterhounds. This breed is one of the most vulnerable breeds out there and is even more endangered than the Giant Panda.[17] The Otterhound (not to be referred to as an Ottie, by the way, as Otterhound owners and breeders tend to be a bit snippy about the cutesy nickname) is a breed that was first bred in England, for the precise purpose of hunting Otters, to prevent fish in stocked ponds and rivers from being consumed by Otters. The behavior of the Otters was of course not unexpected, but the squires and lords in England just weren't inclined to share their fish stocks with Otters, hence the need for Otterhounds. These Otterhounds were created by breeding Bloodhounds, Griffons, and Grand

34   LEARNING LEADERSHIP FROM DOGS

Bleu de Gascogne (another superb breed often called the "King of Hounds" by its proponents), and used in hunting packs to hunt Otters. They produce a wonderful melodic soft howling termed as a Roo (short for A'Roo), which is quite pleasing to listen to, frankly.

These Otterhound packs were extraordinarily successful, which in fact led to a drastic decline in the population of the Otters. As a result, there was legislation passed which banned Otter hunting in 1978. A fictional Otterhound (named Deadlock) was also featured as a villain in the book and subsequent movie, *Tarka the Otter*. That perhaps did a lot of reputational damage to Otterhounds (sort of similar to the reputational damage that *The Lion King* did for dark-maned lions and hyenas.) As a result, Otterhound numbers dwindled significantly, and today, they are sadly one of the most vulnerable breeds out there, with their global numbers estimated at less than 800. Yes, that number is 800, not even a thousand, which accentuates how perilous their position is.

Otterhounds are a large breed and tend to be shaggy, jovial, and dogs with interesting characters. They are also excellent swimmers and do tend to sport perennially wet beards. And to a T, the Otterhound tends to be an agreeable and easygoing dog. I've known many Otterhounds besides Fiona, and they've all been agreeable and kind easy-going dogs (Johnny, Barley, Bella, Mamba, Leeloo, Ozzie, Wicket, etc.) They also possess this innate ability to know when to be gentle and when to be boisterous. True, many dogs could be said to possess that quality, but I've found Otterhounds to be particularly high on this facet. They also appear to unerringly know how to do the right thing. I've seen many of these shaggy powerful dogs become so very gentle when confronted by a young or elderly person. They are also able to sense if someone is afraid of them—instead of bullying and haranguing that individual, instead, they usually attempt to play with them, in a gentle fashion, I must add. That goes a long way in reducing any anxiety or fear on the part of that other individual. These beautiful Hounds somehow always know that is the right thing to do—you can see this in other large breeds like Irish Wolfhounds, Newfoundlands, and many others as well. But, it is a quality far more pronounced in Otterhounds than any other breed I can think of.

We could as humans learn loads from Otterhounds about how exactly to behave with others. Some of us tend to be shyer than the rest—perhaps, the rest of us could take a leaf from the Otterhound book of rules, and do our best to do the right thing, be it in terms of treating other people fairly and with kindness, or in terms of recognizing that sometimes people have anxieties, that they simply cannot control. Yes, sure, one could ignore that person—but wouldn't it be so much more joyous to invite that outsider into the fun? Taking a moral perspective on matters is what authentic leaders do, and from the canine kingdom, I can think of no better breed than the Otterhound to explain how

OTTERLY (O)AUTHENTICITY 35

exactly to do so. And of course, one basically adheres to that principle in a variety of situations that humans deal with—it could be on decisions involving monetary resources. Just remember to be fair, and to use your internal moral marker to make moral and fair decisions. If your internal moral marker is a bit dusty, dust it off, and make it shiny again! Now, let's Roo along to the fourth component of authentic leadership, namely Relational Transparency.

Relational Transparency and Dogs

Relational transparency has to do with the core aspect of authenticity, basically implying that you are thoroughly transparent with others.[3] Instead of hiding behind opaque rules or using iron hands in iron gloves, you take the time to be more transparent about your decisions. This again is a core component of authentic leadership—individuals who hide behind arcane rules and operate mysteriously almost as if they were Death Eaters in the employ of a certain Lord Voldemort, usually display zero relational transparency. That is, of course, desirable if you happen to be a spy or a double agent, but not desirable if you're hoping to motivate your followers.

There are actually several dog breeds that come to mind when it comes to discussing relational transparency. I mean to say, dogs are naturally mostly authentic creatures, so a variety of breeds do fit the bill when it comes to being transparent about how they're feeling. True, there are some breeds which put on an impassive appearance and are a trifle bit guarded in their behavior with others, but there are many more breeds that are transparent than are not. I think one breed, in particular, stands out to me in terms of being very transparent about what the dog wants. I refer to the dynamic Dutch Mastiff. Oh, the breed name is probably causing you to indulge in a bit of head-scratching. That's because very few people call this dog a Dutch Mastiff—they refer to the dog as the Pug, a much-cherished dog.[18] The breed is curiously enough not Dutch nor is it a Mastiff, but the coloring is very similar to the English Mastiff, and I guess, there is a bit of a resemblance. A Dr. Evil and Mini-Me type of comparison could be made, perhaps.

My in-laws have a Pug (named Zeus) who is superbly sweet-tempered, and it must be said needy dog. However, his neediness does not get hidden away— he expresses his desires clearly and without any scope for misunderstanding. If he wants to be picked up, you know it—if he doesn't want to be picked up (pretty rare, let us say!), you know it. A very transparent state of affairs. On the contrary, there's another dog I know (I'm not name-shaming the dog nor the breed), but let us just say, that it feels like you're navigating a minefield with that dog. You never know when a normal movement triggers the dog into an angry fit, and your mind starts feverishly wondering whether there's a nasty bite in the offing.

36 LEARNING LEADERSHIP FROM DOGS

But back to the Pug—this dog is a small and stocky animal, which has a shared ancestry with the Pekingese and the Shih Tzu, through the now-extinct ancient Chinese Happa Dog.[18,19] Today, they are primarily used as companion dogs—they are typically intelligent, cheerful, and outgoing little dogs. And as I mentioned previously, they are incredibly transparent. You know exactly what a Pug is feeling or thinking—they are not international pooches of mystery. The Pug has changed considerably from the nineteenth century to modern times, in that, the current Pugs have much more squished faces than the Pugs of yesteryear. This is mostly due to breeding changes that happen over time, due to changing preferences of dog owners and dog breeders.

Since we're on the topic of companion dogs, I think it only fit to discuss another companion breed here, namely the Chihuahua. This is one of the oldest breeds out there and is likely descended from the indigenous Techichi, which was kept by the indigenous Toltec people originating from Mexico.[20,21] The Chihuahua is the smallest-sized dog among all the dogs out there. It is also one of the most maligned dogs as well, which is oddly enough mostly due to its high relational transparency. Because of its height and size, anything larger than the Chihuahua could be rightfully perceived as dangerous. This perception of others as threats results in snapping and yapping dogs, which then leads people to stereotype them. But if you look at it, they're being completely honest about their innermost feelings—if they feel scared or anxious, better to bark loudly as a deterrent than to go try ignoring their own feelings. In some ways, it's rather ironic that a Chihuahua who is openly letting his or her feelings be known is castigated for doing so. Imagine if you will, that a giant Polar Bear comes running up to you oohing and aahing— wouldn't that make you feel jittery? We're like Polar Bears to such tiny dogs, so it is understandable that they would be cautious around humans, who are all inevitably bigger than the Chihuahua.

Oftentimes, we hear of people getting jittery around dogs who growl when someone approaches them, usually when the dog is eating—many a time, families rehome those dogs because the dog growled at a kid who approached them and tried to take away their bowl of food or what it may be. But the truth is here that the dog authentically and transparently expresses its discomfort, and it's not the dog that needs rehoming, but more the child needing some training (a flippant response would have been to rehome the child, but that would be highly unusual). Chihuahuas are masterful in terms of expressing and displaying their discomfort—it's quite easy to tell what a Chihuahua is feeling because they'll let you know.

They really are brilliant at the relational transparency component of authentic leadership, and we ought to follow a bit of that. Preserving a stiff upper lip at all times is not necessary—it is okay to let genuine expressions follow after feeling or experiencing certain feelings. Of course, better to softly growl than to bite, even as a human.

So, I suppose at this juncture, I must emphasize that the lesson that we can learn from Pugs and Chihuahuas (both prime members of the Companion Dog class) is that we must represent our true selves when interacting with others in our vicinity. Let us not pretend that all is well when all is not in fact well. As leaders, we should not be presenting inauthentic versions of ourselves to our followers and peers—there needs to be a congruence between emotions and expressions. To only display incongruous expressions is disingenuous, and a far cry from being authentic. Chapter 5 will focus on kindness, and I will discuss why it is important for leaders to be kind.

Summary

In this chapter, I discussed and focused on authentic leadership, in particular, the four components of authentic leadership. I also described several breeds of dogs such as the Otterhound, the Collie, and the Pug, among other breeds, who especially fit these authentic leadership components well. In Chapter 5, I will be discussing kindness, and how certain dog breeds are the poster pooches for kindness. I will also discuss why it is important for leaders to be kind in the next chapter.

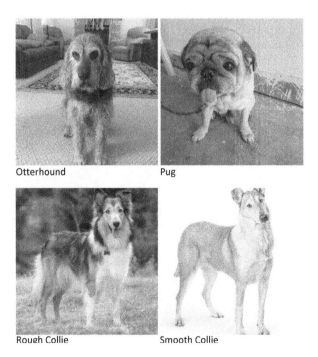

Otterhound   Pug

Rough Collie   Smooth Collie

LEARNING LEADERSHIP FROM DOGS

Labrador Retriever

French Bulldog

Chihuahua

References

1. Avolio, B. J., & Gardner, W. L. (2005). Authentic leadership development: Getting to the root of positive forms of leadership. *The Leadership Quarterly*, 16(3), 315–338.
2. Lehman, D. W., O'Connor, K., Kovács, B., & Newman, G. E. (2019). Authenticity. *Academy of Management Annals*, 13(1), 1–42.
3. Northouse, P. G. (2021). *Leadership: Theory and Practice*. Thousand Oaks, California: Sage Publications.
4. Howell, T. J., & Bennett, P. C. (2011). Can dogs (Canis familiaris) use a mirror to solve a problem? *Journal of Veterinary Behavior*, 6(6), 306–312.
5. Fukuzawa, M., & Hashi, A. (2017). Can we estimate dogs' recognition of objects in mirrors from their behavior and response time? *Journal of Veterinary Behavior*, 17, 1–5.
6. Lenkei, R., Faragó, T., Zsilák, B., & Pongrácz, P. (2021). Dogs (*Canis familiaris*) recognize their own body as a physical obstacle. *Scientific Reports*, 11(1), 2761.
7. https://www.akc.org/dog-breeds/french-bulldog/.
8. https://www.thekennelclub.org.uk/search/breeds-a-to-z/breeds/utility/french-bulldog/#:~:text=Unlike%20other%20Bulldog%20breeds%2C%20the,in%20portraits%20of%20Pa risian%20life.
9. https://tomkingskennel.com/the-fascinating-history-of-french-bulldogs/.
10. https://www.akc.org/dog-breeds/labrador-retriever/.
11. Short, M. (2021). *Histories of the Labrador and the Golden Retriever*. https://guidedogpups.com/2021/03/29/histories-of-the-labrador-retriever-and-the-golden-retriever/.

12 Golan, P. (2009). Collie Shows the Way. The Jerusalem Post. https://www.jpost.com/jerusalem-report/collie-shows-the-way-extract-140434.
13 https://www.thekennelclub.org.uk/search/breeds-a-to-z/breeds/pastoral/collie-rough/.
14 https://www.akc.org/dog-breeds/collie/.
15 McGetrick, J., Peters, H., Korath, A. D., Feitsch, R., Siegmann, S., & Range, F. (2023). Perceived reward attainability may underlie dogs' responses in inequity paradigms. *Scientific Reports*, 13(1), 12066.
16 Horowitz, A. (2012). Fair is fine, but more is better: Limits to inequity aversion in the domestic dog. *Social Justice Research*, 25, 195–212.
17 Kline, W.R. (n.d.) https://www.otterhounduniversity.com/history.html.
18 https://pugdogpassion.com/happa-lo-tze-chinese-pugs-the-chinese-origin/.
19 https://www.akc.org/dog-breeds/pug/.
20 https://www.britannica.com/animal/Chihuahua-dog.
21 https://www.akc.org/dog-breeds/chihuahua/.

Chapter 5

KINGLY KINDNESS

A quote by Maya Angelou which I keep seeing on people's walls, talks about how people remember how you made them feel instead of the specifics of what you actually said or did. I am absolutely on board and in concordance with the meaning of that quote. One may or may not remember specifics, but one always remembers if someone was kind to them. And, there is no doubt in my mind that kindness matters and has a whole host of possibilities attached to it. Take a moment and think about someone in your life whom you always remember fondly and picture that person in your mind. Think about whether that person was kind to you. I'm fairly confident that a majority of people who do that will pick someone who was kind to them.

Sadly, kindness is not an attribute that one associates much with leaders or leadership. You rarely find someone professing to be a kind leader—usually, they'll insist that they are hardworking and performance driven or some other such attribute. I believe that a case could be made for leaders to instead focus on being kind leaders, as their kindness could have both direct and indirect effects on their followers and even the organizations that they lead. Of course, like everything in life, being kind does not mean that you should be a pushover. Kind is not a synonym for being a doormat, but I'll explain that in a bit more detail further on in the chapter.

Now on to our pooch pals—kindness is perhaps one of the biggest attributes or qualities one can learn from dogs. I could honestly fit in a hundred different breeds right here in this very chapter, but one must pace oneself. No point in bunding all the breeds into one huge chapter—that wouldn't be very kind, would it? Let me start off by describing the first dog that comes to mind when I think of the word "Kindness." Just a little explanation for this chapter's title—a lot of the dogs I'll refer to in this chapter hail from royal backgrounds, that is, they originally were only meant for royal families to possess, so it makes sense to refer to the royal pedigree in the title.

Newfoundlands and Kindness

It wouldn't be too much of a spoiler now, seeing that the heading has already given it away, to state that the Newfoundland is for me, the poster dog for kindness. Newfoundlands are a beautiful giant breed that also descended from the St. John's Water Dog in Canada.[1,2] However, when compared with their Labrador Retriever cousins, the Newfoundlands are significantly larger. These dogs can weigh almost 150 pounds when they're fully grown and are unparalleled water rescue dogs. One wouldn't be too far off to call them the Saint Bernards of the water (although they are indeed two completely separate dog breeds). The Newfoundland is perhaps the kindest dog out there. Kind and gentle with their family, and kind and gentle with other dogs, as well as strangers. That doesn't mean they're pushovers though—if a stranger means harm to their family, the Newfoundland will not turn tail and run, but will instead protect its family.

Like its cousins the Labrador Retrievers, Newfoundlands are water dogs.[2] And their temperament is similar too—sweetness of temperament is considered to be a breed standard. Newfoundlands typically come in three primary colors, Black, Black and White called Landseer, and Brown. Apart from the different coat colors, all three types are almost identical. For Peter Pan fans, you will recollect that Nana was a Newfoundland, more specifically a Landseer variety (the Black and White ones).[3] That actually has led Newfoundlands to be referred to as Nanny dogs, because of the way they are so gentle and caring toward children. There are also umpteen incidents where Newfoundlands have helped rescue people struggling in a body of water. Although, there is one case that highlights the mischievous nature that all dogs have—there is a somewhat apocryphal but still amusing incident of a Newfoundland in France back in 1910, which got into the habit of gently pushing children into the Seine and then promptly rescuing them, in order to receive a reward (usually a delicious steak of some sort).[4,5] But that is an unusual case—typically, Newfoundlands would never dream of doing anything like that. Of course, it is also possible that the news itself was highly exaggerated. Another dog breed that comes to mind when thinking about kindness is the playful yet boisterous Boxer.

Boxers and Kindness

Boxers are a breed that is amazingly kind—they are so patient and so wonderful with young children. Do yourself a favor, and hop onto YouTube, and search for videos of Boxers and babies. Well, you may have to parse through them a bit because some of the videos are bound to feature human

KINGLY KINDNESS

pugilists and children, but you'll eventually find videos of Boxer dogs with babies. Here's an example of one such video.[6] Those videos or snippets will show you exactly what I mean when I talk about the kindness of Boxers. The patience that manifestly shows itself in Boxers is astounding to the max! Let's learn a bit more about Boxers now, shall we?

These dogs are instantly recognizable due to the way they actually "box" when playing with other dogs or humans. They often stand on their hind legs and make movements that resemble boxing jabs. This behavior is often credited with being the reason for the dog's name, but sources have suggested that it is merely a charming tale to add to the mythos of the breed's history. The Boxer is a breed that originates in Germany and is possibly descended from breeds like the Great Dane and the Bulldog. It was originally bred to be a bullbaiting dog, just like the Bulldog, but was also used for farm work and hunting (especially of wild boar). Today of course, the Boxer still finds employment as a law enforcement and military dog, but is also equally at home being a family pet. As I mentioned earlier, the Boxer is just brilliantly kind with children, and yet, not a milquetoast so as to be useless in matters of protection.

The fashion sense of yore dictated that Boxer tails be docked, however, that practice appears to be luckily fading away. However, it still appears to be unregulated in the US, while it is banned in Australia, the UK, and several countries in Europe. The AKC appears to differ from the American Veterinary Medical Association (AVMA) in terms of whether or not Boxer tails should be docked.[7,8] But either way, docked or undocked, the Boxer is a dog that you can entrust your family including your young children to, without any worries. Kindness is a virtue that goes a long way, in terms of engendering trust.

Irish Wolfhounds and Kindness

I have always had a very soft spot in my heart for the amazing Irish Wolfhounds. This dog breed is the tallest breed among all—on occasion, some Great Danes may be bigger than the Irish Wolfhounds, but generally speaking, Irish Wolfhounds tower over the rest of the canine kingdom. This is another ancient breed and has been known in Ireland for thousands of years.[9,10] In the beginning, they were reserved for only nobility, that included Irish royalty, and the members of royal families from other countries. The royals from other countries would often get gifted an Irish Wolfhound as a present. A historical tidbit here is that Oliver Cromwell in 1652 announced a ban on the gifting away of Irish Wolfhounds to foreign parts, primarily because the worry was that the wolf population would rebound in a dramatic

44 LEARNING LEADERSHIP FROM DOGS

fashion.[11] Hey, this could well be a million-dollar question on one of those Who Wants to be a Millionaire type of shows, or at least worth its weight in gold at the local pub's trivia night.

The Irish Wolfhound is a sight hound and typical of sight hounds relies on its speed and athletic build. They were traditionally used for hunting wolves and elk, but after the gray wolf became extinct in Ireland in 1786, the Wolfhound itself teetered on the brink of extinction. In 1870, thanks to pioneering rescue work by Captain George A. Graham of the British Army, the Irish Wolfhound was saved from becoming extinct. We all owe a lot of gratitude to Captain Graham for having spearheaded the program to revive the Irish Wolfhound—it would have been a huge loss for such a historically important breed. Thankfully the breed has survived and is also one of the regimental mascots for the Irish Guards (a regiment from the British Army, that protects the Royal Family of England).

Now on to kindness—the Irish Wolfhound contrary to what its name might conjure is not a fierce and destructive breed. Instead, it happens to be one of the gentlest dogs out there. The Irish Wolfhound makes an amazing gentle companion dog and apart from a shockingly aberrant incident in New Zealand,[12] the Irish Wolfhound has never been involved in any sort of aggression toward other humans or dogs. There is an ancient Welsh legend about Gelert, a favored Irish Wolfhound owned by a certain Prince Llewellyn the Great. Legend has it that when Llewellyn returned from a hunt, he saw Gelert with blood on his mouth, and he saw that his baby (i.e. the Prince's baby) was missing. He jumped to a hasty conclusion and unjustly killed Gelert—after finding his baby alive near a dead wolf, he was grief-stricken. As a result, he had Gelert buried with a memorial stone, and today, you can see a sculpture of Gelert near his grave in Beddgelert, Wales. By the by, the name Beddgelert literally means Grave of Gelert in Welsh. Again, as is the case, in so many legends, the story may be slightly exaggerated for effect, but there is no denying that it is entirely within the realm of possibility. At any rate, it might be well worth a visit to picturesque Beddgelert, to take a picture with Gelert's sculpture,[13] even if the story surrounding it is a tad bit ornate and embellished.

The Irish Wolfhound (the reason I keep using the word Irish in front of Wolfhound, is that there are other varieties of Wolfhounds, such as the Borzoi, etc.) is absolutely another sublimely kind dog, and if we could somehow follow its lead and be calmer and kinder, it would be such a solid improvement of our own personalities. I will be next diving into how exactly, one can go about inculcating kindness. But prior to doing that, I do wish to discuss a few other breeds which fit the bill, when it comes to kindness. There is a somewhat strongly held stereotype that large breeds are kinder and gentler than small

KINGLY KINDNESS   45

or toy breeds. That is somewhat true because large breeds usually are a lot more forgiving if someone accidentally steps on them or bumps into them, while a toy breed may bite in the same situation. That's a given because the toy or small breed dog is at greater risk of getting hurt if someone steps on them, so a resultant warning growl or a bite is more likely from a small breed than a large or giant breed. However, there are still plenty of beautiful and supremely kind smaller and even toy breeds out there, that we could all do with taking a cue from.

Smaller Dog Breeds and Kindness

When it comes to smaller dog breeds and kindness, the first one that comes to mind, well at least my mind, is the King Charles Spaniel and its close relative the Cavalier King Charles Spaniel. Now you may find these two names a bit puzzling, and they honestly are puzzling, since they're so similar sounding. But there are important differences between the two breeds. The biggest difference is in terms of size—the Cavalier King Charles Spaniels are bigger than the King Charles Spaniels, and they're also more recent.[14,15] The former breed was basically bred to closely resemble the dogs favored by King Charles himself. People also call the regular King Charles Spaniels as English Toy Spaniels, but most dog fanciers refer to the breed as King Charles Spaniels. Both varieties of Spaniels are affectionate and incredibly kind dogs. They are well-behaved to a fault and very loving dogs. The stereotypical thinking that small dogs are always yapping about and creating drama totally falls apart when confronted by either variety of the King Charles Spaniels.

The King Charles Spaniel most likely descended from small Chinese and Japanese breeds. However, they've been around in England, especially the Royal courts since the sixteenth century. These dogs come in a variety of color patterns too, with the most common types being black and tan, and red and white. These dogs are also wonderful companions—I have yet to come across a King Charles Spaniel who was rowdy or vicious. They are the epitome of gentleness and kindness.

Another small breed that epitomizes kindness is the Coton de Tulear.[16] This beautiful happy dog is called the Royal Dog of Madagascar, and the name "Coton" basically refers to its fluffy soft white coat, which resembles cotton. Coton owners swear by the amazing awareness that Cotons display—essentially, they describe Cotons as being incredibly astute in picking up on the emotions of their owners. Of course, many other dogs are equally accomplished at doing so, but Cotons have this sympathetic air to them, that is a Coton trademark of sorts. The Coton de Tulear is a dog that hails from

46 LEARNING LEADERSHIP FROM DOGS

the Bichon family, with other members including Bichon Frise, Bolognese, Maltese, Havanese, among others.

There is another legend of sorts which is attached to the Coton de Tulear. Since Madagascar has an abundant supply of Nile Crocodiles, swimming around in the rivers or walking through the watery stretches to get to another land area is a task that is fraught with risk. According to the legendary tale,[17] the Cotons found a way to do so safely—apparently, one of the Cotons would bark loudly at the crocodiles, thus causing the crocodiles to pay attention to it, while the rest of the Coton pack made their escape through the narrowest path of the crossing. Once, the pack was through, the remaining Coton would also quickly run back to that point and make its escape. Definitely, the tale seems a bit fishy or embellished to me, as gutsy or not, I think crossing a stream with Nile Crocodiles around is a tough proposition.

Regardless of the tale's veracity, the Coton de Tulear has its head screwed on well. This is an intelligent and gentle dog, which happens to be great with other dogs and other humans too. Its endearing kindness is a quality that really comes to the forefront. Now let's move on to talking about how kindness can be taught and learned. It's important to do both, of course.

How Do You Inculcate Kindness?

The preceding sections of this chapter focused on several breeds that I consider to be synonymous with kindness. There are many other breeds of course, but then we run the risk of having this chapter being rather bloated. So, let's shift gears and dive into the sparkly realm of kindness. How does one go about teaching kindness? It's easy to tell someone to be kind, but it isn't easy to actually do. One of the primary elements of kindness is to recognize that someone may need a generous dose of kindness. It sounds a bit like emotional intelligence or specifically empathy, and indeed, empathetic persons often tend to be kind persons. How do empathetic persons operate? They basically put themselves into the shoes of the other person and think about the situation from the other's perspective. Avoid being judgmental, and instead consider the situation from the other person's unique position.

It is a trifle bit hard to do of course—we all usually are trained and equipped to handle situations from our own point-of-view, and it's the rare soul among us, who always considers other's positions prior to making decisions. Taking on the other's perspective is of course an easy lesson to learn from dogs, as they definitely do that. All of the breeds I discussed previously do so, and many more breeds do so as well. Our dogs are always observing us, and they are keenly attuned to how we're feeling, and our dogs probably have a better sense of our emotions than we do ourselves. I know when I'm personally agitated or feeling anxious, Fiona (my pet Otterhound) always seems to know and comes silently up to me to let me know that whatever the matter is, it isn't an insurmountable issue. I bet that most if not all of you reading this who happen to have dogs in your family will have had moments like that yourselves. Sometimes, all it takes to be kind is to be available for the person who maybe needs something to hold on to, to help regain composure.

Let's consider a hypothetical example here, and one that many of us may have faced at one time or another—let's say someone steals your lunch sandwich or your personal food at work from the communal refrigerator. Obviously, your first reaction is going to be anger or at least annoyance. An empathetic way to think about this would be to consider that perhaps the lunchroom pilferer is truly in desperate circumstances and was forced to steal your food. A truly kind response would be to pack an extra sandwich for that individual, as opposed to raising hell and hiring a convoy of private investigators to discover the perpetrator of the ghastly crime. Of course, if the individual steals both sandwiches the next time around, then you know that being kind is not really the optimal course of action here, and it may be time to call on the services of Miss Marple or Hercule Poirot. This does of course depend on the severity of the transgression—if instead of the sandwich, the pilferer was stealing company trademark secrets and hawking them to the highest bidder, then it is probably wiser to dispense with the kindness and focus on the consequences side of the equation.

I have found in my own experience that the best way to inculcate kindness is to actually model it yourself. Be kind to others, and a majority of those folks will return the favor back to you. Yes, you are bound to eventually meet the ungrateful cynical kinds who will exploit your kindness. The trick to dealing with that motley crew is to not let their unkindness rub off on you. If your modeling kindness doesn't work on some people, then let it be. Move along and model it with others who are more receptive to kindness. Modeling kindness is not 100% guaranteed to increase kindness, but it at least does work wonders on a vast majority of people. Leaders too will find many beneficial outcomes when they model kindness and behave kindly toward their followers and colleagues. The biggest benefit is of course loyalty—most people would want to be loyal to a company or a boss who treats them with kindness. That loyalty will have so many ripple effects throughout the company, including lesser absenteeism, more citizenship behaviors, more collaboration, and so on. All of that kindness basically goes a long way in providing lasting benefits for all. I will next discuss one solid and absolutely workable way by which you can model kindness.

Mentor the Way with Kindness

Sometimes, there may be situations in life, where we all may feel the need for someone who could personally guide us through that situation. The situation could be professional or personal, but regardless of its origin, the need for some help at that critical juncture is felt by many. That's where mentorship comes into play. Mentoring someone and looking out for someone to help them grow professionally or personally is one of the kindest acts any individual could perform.[18] Yes, it takes a lot to mentor another person—it is hard work and should not be attempted half-heartedly. If you're unable to be fully committed to your mentee, then don't even bother becoming a mentor. It is far kinder to not lead someone on but to instead make it clear that perhaps a mentor–mentee relationship is not feasible.

I have found that the act of mentoring someone is such an intimate bond—you have the ability to make a difference in that other person's life. Perhaps, you can be the reason for that person choosing a certain career track or trajectory. And perhaps, you can be the stability in that person's life. There are many ways by which a person can become a mentor. One way is of course to be receptive to cold calls. Sometimes, you might end up getting a stranger who sends you an email or a connection request on LinkedIn and expresses a desire to be mentored by you. If you have the availability to do so, why not take a bit of time and see if there would be a fit? And of course, you can also join up in formal networking events, where the organizers have mentoring opportunities. I've done that in the past and continue to do so in the present and the future too, where I've mentored several first-generation students. And, many of those students have gone on to completing graduate degrees, and are thriving professionally. Some other business leaders I know (i.e., CEOs and CFOs) give back so much of their time and effort in mentoring others, and they too tell me that they thoroughly enjoy the process of mentorship.

Dogs actually do this all the time—I refer to mentoring. If you have an older dog, and then get a new puppy. Watch how the older dog often takes on the task of "training" the puppy, getting the puppy housebroken, and getting the puppy to be a well-behaved pup. You don't have to even become a formal mentor—being an informal mentor is good enough. Let's say you work at an organization, and a new hire comes along. It may be a bit of a bother to assist the newcomer in so many aspects that they may need assistance in. After all, assisting a newcomer takes away time from your own duties, and probably lengthens the amount of time it takes for you to get through your day. But, by taking the time to help the newcomer and possibly mentor the newcomer, you are ensuring a potentially loyal

KINGLY KINDNESS 49

and useful person, who will return the kindness back to you manifold in the future (again, most likely—sometimes people can be total ingrates). And even if it turns out that there is nothing gained for you, perhaps, your kindness to that individual will lead that individual to be kind to someone else. Hence, a climate that ushers in an air of kindness for all can begin to be established and even thrive. I will next discuss how to avoid getting your kindness to be taken advantage of.

Mind your Kind(ness)

A lot of what I've discussed previously basically boils down to being kind to others, and that kindness then goes on to influence those individuals to be kind to others. However, as I hinted in several spots previously, sometimes kindness gets taken advantage of. Some people are opportunists and immune to feeling a sense of gratitude. That category of people could be termed as political or Machiavellian[19] to the core because they only ever do something if they benefit from it. We are likely to run into someone like that at some point in our lives and careers. But we should not let those bitter experiences jade us and turn us bitter or cynical after all, kindness is a virtue, and if someone chooses not to be influenced by it, let it be. Getting influenced adversely by them and changing your own personality is not worth it in the slightest. Sure, it feels a bit bitter, but treat it as a life lesson, and just move along.

In the discussion about specific dog breeds that are incredibly kind, some astute readers may wonder why I didn't mention Golden Retrievers at all. The reason for that is Golden Retrievers are perhaps the friendliest and kindest dogs out there, but the kindness they are known for goes a bit too far. They are wholly unsuitable as guard dogs—if a burglar comes calling to your house in your absence, there is every likelihood that your Golden Retriever will retrieve the family jewels to spare the burglar the trouble of searching for them. The Boxer or the Newfoundland, and so on, will not be quite as kind as the Golden Retriever. So, when I say, be kind, I mean be kind with a limit to your kindness. If your kindness is being reciprocated with cruel indifference, then obviously put an end to limitless kindness.

Being kind should not be an invitation to others to treat you poorly. You have to learn to stand up for yourself at a point, preferably as soon as you notice that your kindness is being taken advantage of—kindness should not equate to your being a milquetoast or a doormat.

This is where some of the points discussed in the chapter on communication come into prominence—you must absolutely make it clear to the other person that you can see that they are not responding well to your kindness, so you must cease showering them with your kindness or kind actions. Essentially, at that point, I would suggest being kind to yourself.

Nobody deserves to be taken advantage of or treated cruelly, least of all, someone who is striving to be kind. Be kind to yourself as well. This is actually a great segue to the next chapter, which is going to be all about Respect!

Summary

This chapter discusses kindness, how one can strive to be kind, and why one needs to be kind. I also discuss the pitfalls of bestowing unlimited kindness on others, especially those who do not seem to appreciate receiving kindness. In this chapter, I discussed dog breeds like the Boxer, Newfoundland, Coton de Tulear, Irish Wolfhound, and both kinds of King Charles Spaniels. In Chapter 6, I will discuss why it is paramount for leaders to be respectful and to establish climates and cultures of respect, and also describe certain dog breeds that exemplify respect.

Irish Wolfhound

Newfoundland

Boxer

KINGLY KINDNESS

King Charles Spaniel

Coton de Tulear

Golden Retriever

Cavalier King Charles Spaniel

References

1. https://mybrownnewfies.com/2019/07/09/do-newfoundlands-make-good-family-dogs/.
2. https://www.akc.org/dog-breeds/newfoundland/.
3. https://www.thenewfoundland.org/nana.html.
4. https://www.nytimes.com/1908/02/02/archives/dog-a-fake-hero-pushes-children-into-the-seine-to-rescue-them-and.html.
5. https://www.iflscience.com/the-dog-who-kept-pushing-kids-into-a-river-to-acquire-steak-rewards-62917.
6. https://www.youtube.com/watch?v=uvNZHnSIZKY.
7. https://www.akc.org/press-releases/akc-statement-on-avma-crop-and-dock-policy/.
8. https://www.avma.org/resources-tools/animal-health-and-welfare/animal-welfare/canine-tail-docking-faq.
9. https://www.akc.org/dog-breeds/irish-wolfhound/.
10. https://www.thekennelclub.org.uk/search/breeds-a-to-z/breeds/hound/irish-wolfhound/.
11. https://www.akc.org/expert-advice/dog-breeds/irish-wolfhound-history-behind-the-breed/.
12. https://www.irishcentral.com/news/irish-wolfhounds-viciously-attack-new-zealand-woman.
13. https://www.beddgelerttourism.com/Gelert/.
14. https://www.akc.org/dog-breeds/cavalier-king-charles-spaniel/.

15 https://www.thekennelclub.org.uk/search/breeds-a-to-z/breeds/toy/king-charles-spaniel/.

16 https://www.akc.org/dog-breeds/coton-de-tulear/.

17 https://akc.org/expert-advice/dog-breeds/coton-de-tulear-history-madagascars-feral-fluffy-dogs/.

18 Freedman, M. (1999). *The Kindness of Strangers: Adult Mentors, Urban Youth, and the New Voluntarism*. Francisco: Jossey-Bass.

19 Carré, J. R., Jones, D. N., & Mueller, S. M. (2020). Perceiving opportunities for legal and illegal profit: Machiavellianism and the Dark Triad. *Personality and Individual Differences*, 162, 109942.

Chapter 6

ROTTIE RESPECT

This topic was earlier slated for a later appearance and was going to saunter in as Chapter 9 in this book. However, seeing a natural fit with Chapter 5, I decided to focus this chapter on respect instead. Respect is a virtue that seems to be increasingly waning in this world of ours. People seem to be experiencing a lot of incivility at work and elsewhere, and a lack of respect seems to be getting to being endemic across societies.[1-3] That does not auger well for the future of our overall civilization, as respect is the grease that helps propel the wheels of civilization. Cooperation and coworking go a long way further if respect is along for the ride. This absolutely applies in the workplace as well as in personal life. Leaders who are respectful find that their followers are respectful too, and sometimes, this works vice versa as well.

In this chapter, I will focus my explanation and discussion on how one can be respectful, and how one can command respect. You need both for optimal mileage—while it is important to be respectful to others, it is equally important for you to be able to command respect as well. Just like kindness, there is no point in being sublimely respectful in the midst of appalling disrespect. Limitless respect like limitless kindness in the face of disrespect or unkindness has no benefit for any individual, be it a leader or a non-leader.

Dogs absolutely fill in these two dimensions of respect really well. For instance, there are some dog breeds that inspire respect. When someone looks at certain breeds, they will automatically give those dogs respect. The appearance and history of those breeds dictate that respect is a given, when interacting with these dogs. The old chestnut about "Size Matters" actually does weigh in here considerably. And then, there are dogs that are respectful to the hilt—the polite lot, who are simply stunningly respectful in all their interactions. Sometimes, you have breeds that fit both descriptions, but of course, but for the purposes of this chapter, I'm going to focus on adhering to a demarcation of the two. Let's start off with the lot who inspire respect from others. In this category, I'm actually going to be further demarcating it into two more categories, one of which deals with a heavy dosage of fear. Finally, I will also have a brief discussion of what exactly current leaders or future leaders can take away from all of the other discussion and description.

Respect Me

There are some dogs who one simply cannot help but respect. A lot of times, it's because of the role these dogs play, and in some cases, it's more to do with the general history of the breed. But regardless of why, the fact is that some dog breeds command respect. Let me discuss the first one that comes to mind, yes indeed, this breed is the breed referred to in the title of this chapter, namely the Rottweiler, sometimes lovingly referred to as a Rottie.[4,5] This breed commands respect straight off the bat. Part of the reason is of course that the media has demonized the breed a lot due to some bad owners and their (typically abused) dogs having been involved in attacks on innocent dogs or humans. However, despite its rather fearsome reputation thanks to the press, responsible owners of Rottweilers know that this is a dog that is ultra-sweet with its family and a very forgiving and sweet family pet. So, let's embark on a quick discussion about the Rottweiler.

The Rottweiler traces its lineage from ancient Asian Mastiffs that were brought into Germany by the Romans when the Roman army brought those dogs along to drive cattle, which they'd bring with them on their marches and invasions.[4,5] As the name suggests, the modern-day Rottweiler hails from the town of Rottweil in Germany. Rotties have been used in a plethora of occupations, from herding and driving cattle to hunting bears to pulling carts as butchers' dogs. In fact, there they ended up with the name Rottweiler Metzerhund or the Butcher's Dog of Rottweil. They would also of course protect cattle and people from bandits and cattle rustlers. This particular occupation was disrupted once the railroads took off in the 1800s.

After that Rottweilers have been used as police dogs and protection dogs, and of course, some don't work anymore apart from entertaining their families. But given its impressive and imposing physical structure, can there be any other dog more deserving of respect? Most outsiders looking at a Rottweiler would automatically give the Rottie respect. On a related note, guess which human occupation typically automatically obtains respect. Well yes, I suppose, law enforcement and military occupations come first to most people's minds, but as the famous song by The Beatles suggests, the Taxman (or Tax Collector) is one occupation that people simply can't help but respect (even if not joyously). The reason I bring the Taxman up is that there is a dog breed that commands respect, and the origins of that dog are intractably associated with a tax collector. I refer to the Dobermann Pinscher sometimes called the Doberman Pinscher or simply the Dobermann.[6,7]

The Dobermann (or Dobie for its admirers) is a dog breed that was developed in the late nineteenth century by a German Tax Collector named Louis Dobermann. He created a dog that was to protect him and other tax

ROTTIE RESPECT

collectors. He developed the new breed from various dogs like the German Shepherd, German Pinscher, Rottweiler, etc. That led to the dog being named the Dobermann Pinscher. In current times, the Pinscher has been dropped from the name in most countries except for the US and Canada—so now, it's simply called the Dobermann elsewhere, but called the Doberman Pinscher in the US and Canada. Just some contrariness, I suppose! A bit of contrariness makes the world more interesting.

The Dobermann is a strikingly handsome dog, and yet, bears the burden of possessing an unjustified reputation of being an aggressive and dangerous dog. Of course, that unjustified reputation has to do with media and popular culture representations (e.g., the Resident Evil series have a zombified Dobermann in them). However, the instincts of the Dobermann as a protection dog have not waned away. They are one of the most loyal and protective breeds out there, and that should not be confounded with aggression. One can be protective without being aggressive, and similarly, one should naturally command respect without being a bully about it. Leaders should command respect naturally, and not bully people disrespectfully to gain respect—that sort of respect is of the grudging sort, which is neither authentic nor sustainable. At one point or the other, that sort of respect will fade away as a snowflake would under the glare of the midday sun. Both the Rottweiler and the Dobermann are dogs that provide a great sort of template for us to follow, to make sure that we receive sustainable respect from others too.

Since docking our tails is out of the question, the only way to really work on obtaining respect from others is to work on our reputations. Deliver results and work hard may sound like a pithy chestnut, but it goes really well with what the Rottweiler and Dobermann stand for.

Another category of dog breeds that command respect simply due to their imposing physical size is dogs from the Molossus family, or as they're called now, the Mastiff family. Most Mastiffs tend to be massive, with the exception of The Dutch Mastiff (which as you will recall was the lovable yet diminutive Pug). The name Mastiff while sounding similar to massive does not exactly mean that. Apparently, the term comes from the word "Masty," which means powerful. Either way, the word Mastiff usually refers to massive dogs—most Mastiff varieties are either large or giant dogs. Let's start off with the biggest of them all—the English Mastiff, which is simply called the Mastiff.[8,9]

The English Mastiff is another old British breed which has been around for centuries now. They were used as "dogs of war" and also as protectors of homes and livestock. These dogs can weigh from 175 to 190 pounds and are immensely powerful dogs. A burglar who breaks into a house and confronts a Mastiff will most likely get a massive shock at the sight. But if the burglar

56 LEARNING LEADERSHIP FROM DOGS

knows anything about dogs, I suppose he'll know that Mastiffs are calm and gentle dogs. They don't look gentle but they are gentle. But they do command respect—the burglar in our example from above, would probably doff his hat to the Mastiff, and quietly make his way out without stealing a penny from the house. The Mastiff is amazing as a family pet—honestly, the only big drawback that I can think about having a Mastiff is its enormity. They will need a lot of space, so if you presently live in a small studio apartment or something, perhaps go get a Dutch Mastiff instead.

Another Mastiff variety is the Neapolitan Mastiff,[10,11] straight from Naples, Italy. The Neapolitan Mastiff is considered as the national mastiff of Italy. The Neapolitan Mastiff is not as big as its English counterpart, but they too can get to be about 150 pounds or so. They are also quite massive, and an Italian burglar would also get a similarly large shock to come across one of the Mastinos (a nickname for the breed) during a brazen act of burglary. Fans of Harry Potter will recognize Hagrid's "Boar Hound" as a Neapolitan Mastiff. In reality, I suppose, the makers should have used a Great Dane to play Fang, but they probably liked the look of the Neapolitan Mastiff better, since the body type of the latter breed suited Hagrid better than the thinner Great Dane. This is another dog that simply cannot but help be respected—its sheer size and appearance dictate that respect naturally be bestowed on it.

All of the dogs I've talked about in this section fall into the category of breeds that just by dint of appearance compel people to respect them. A corollary of that for humans suggests that there are things we can do to get others to respect us. The first aspect to think of concerns demeanor—all of the dogs mentioned above possess a sharp and calm demeanor. That does matter—the ability to be calm despite trying circumstances helps accentuate your image to others and compels them to respect you. Now I'm going to discuss some dog breeds that pretty much demand respect as without respect they will provide consequences.

Respect Me [...] You Had Better!

Now there are some dogs that frequently make into the ranks of dogs that are banned by apartment or house landlords. In some cases, municipalities ban these dogs. Ostensibly, the ban is supposed to be based on bite incidences, media reporting, and potential dangers of the breed. Now granted that some breeds on these lists are just there due to reporters' zealous frenzy, but there is no denying that some of these dog breeds veer into problematic and dangerous dog breed zones. However, this also augers well from a respect point of view. Let me start off with the Fila Brasileiro.[12,13]

ROTTIE RESPECT

This is a huge Brazilian Mastiff, which has a strong resemblance to a Bloodhound because the latter line was bred to develop these dogs. The Fila is no longer recognized by AKC, as the dog has such a strong protective instinct, that it would never let a stranger (let alone a hapless AKC judge) handle it. Indeed, in the case of the Fila Brasileiro, if a dog displays fear of any sort, then that is a shortcoming in that particular dog. This dog is powerful and takes no nonsense from anyone. This is not a dog that brooks disrespect of any sort, and indeed, can and does remind us of leaders who act just like that. You really have to be on your toes a lot—this is not to say that Filas are bad dogs. It's just they've been bred for a certain purpose (i.e., to guard large estates), and they need to be tough and fearless dogs. This is a dog that you disrespect at your own peril.

Another dog that falls into a similar category is the Japanese Tosa.[14] Bigger Tosas can weigh up to 198 pounds, and this is a dog breed that should not be kept or handled by regular lackadaisical owners or handlers. The Tosa was used as a fighting breed in Japan, and indeed, in Japan, the Tosa is considered the canine equivalent of Sumo wrestlers. Nobody but a person who lacks sense of any sort would consider it a worthwhile pursuit to disrespect a Sumo wrestler—the same admonition exists for the Tosa. This breed also shows up on many a banned breed list across countries. To be fair though, the Tosa gets along well with its own family—it's only with other dogs that the dog is rather unreliable. That can make it a big challenge to go to parks or walks. I suppose that's why traditionally people with large estates would have this dog as well.

Next, let's talk about the Dogo Argentino.[15] As the name suggests, this is a breed that originates from Argentina. It was chiefly bred to hunt large game, and it's a strikingly handsome dog. It is completely white, and the large game that it was bred to hunt included wild boar, pumas, and peccaries. While this breed is not as fierce as the Fila or the Tosa, it can be mighty destructive if in the wrong hands. Again, respect if not given to the Dogo, can result in many nasty bites being delivered with impunity to the disrespectful lot. The Dogo Argentino also does not brook any disrespect, and its immense power and history make it a fool's errand to treat it with anything but respect.

Another dog that I absolutely must mention here is the Presa Canario.[16] This is a massive Spanish dog originating from the Canary Islands. While this one too is not as big as the English Mastiff or even the Japanese Tosa or the Fila Brasileiro, it is still a physically imposing dog. The Presa Canario is usually very docile and loving with its immediate family, but naturally suspicious of strangers. This can be a problem because a poorly trained Presa Canario can be quite deadly. This is similar to another dog called the Cane Corso.[17]

58 LEARNING LEADERSHIP FROM DOGS

The Cane Corso is an Italian Mastiff, and albeit on the smaller side is still fairly a large dog. Both the Presa Canario and Cane Corsos also tend to appear on many a banned list!

Part of the reason is that bad owners, who should not be allowed to own even a stuffed Pochita or Snoopy toy get these massive and strong-willed dogs, and don't train or control them properly. As a result of these irresponsible dog owners, so many dog breeds get unfairly tarnished with a bad reputation, and end up on banned dog breed lists, thus earning permanent notoriety. The Staffordshire Bull Terrier and other variants of that dog also get featured with regularity on such lists. So, in a sense, there is notoriety but that does come with respect, although the respect is tinged with fear.

If I had to contrast this set of dogs with the dogs mentioned in the previous section, I think the chief difference between the two sets of dogs is that the latter set generates a whole lot of fear which is tied to how much respect they get. The former group of dogs also can be scary for folks who're afraid of dogs, but frankly, if you compare a Fila Brasileiro with an English Mastiff, the latter will be a lot less scarier to hang out with. Of course, that does depend on how much knowledge you have of dogs. If you know nothing about dogs, then even a Newfoundland will look scary. But basically, my point in discussing these two categories of dogs was to emphasize that while both categories of dogs are worthy of respect by dint of their size, one category of dog breeds is a lot more-riskier to be disrespectful to.

Leaders are just like that—you could probably get away with publicly questioning (or challenging) a democratically elected political leader or a fairly open-to-feedback leader, but imagine doing that to a bona fide dictator. Or from the business world, imagine doing that to someone like Elon Musk or Vince McMahon or some other such authoritarian-type business leader. While those authoritarian leaders are respected, a lot of that respect has more to do with fear than it does purely respect for respect's sake. The same principle applies when it comes to some of the dogs I've discussed in the chapter up to this point. There is indubitably respect involved when it comes to dealing with Mastiffs or Dogo Argentinos, but in some cases, the respect is probably out of fear. While fear can be useful to generate respect, I don't know if it's the kind of respect leaders should be aiming for. I believe the respect that comes without fear associated with it is the far more sustainable and beneficial kind of respect. I'm now going to discuss certain dog breeds who you can't help respecting either, and it's not even out of fear of any sort. That is the kind of respect one really ought to aim for as leaders—let's tally ho, and move to the next section.

Respect Me [...]. Pretty Please

There are some dogs that have excellent manners and are as polite as can be. And there are dogs that obviously showcase pride and carry themselves with regality. Both those qualities can lead people to automatically grant them respect. Of course, here I could probably wax eloquence about the politeness of Fiona here (my Otterhound), but then that rather defeats the purpose, of being able to identify and describe other dog breeds. Let's start off with one of the politest dogs out there, the Bloodhound.[18,19] As a kid, I remember another kid recounting tales about a Bloodhound, which for all purposes seemed more like a bloodthirsty creature from one of Count Dracula's castles. After that, I read up about Bloodhounds, and the next time, I saw that fibber, I made sure to tell him that his entire tale was fake. The Bloodhound is one of the gentlest dogs out there and is such a beautiful breed. Amiable and great company to be with and also possibly the dog with the best nose out there. The Scent Hound of all scent hounds is the Bloodhound.

This ancient breed is not called the Bloodhound because of some sort of grotesque obsessive fascination with blood, as the youthful fibber from my past made it out to be. It is called the Bloodhound because it's short for "blooded hounds," which refers to their aristocratic background. The Bloodhound's nose is said to be the most superior nose in the entire canine kingdom, and indeed, possibly on Earth itself. They never give up if on a trail and will pursue their quarry (be it an escaped prisoner or a child who's lost in the great outdoors) till they finally locate that individual. In fact, the Bloodhound is the only dog breed whose evidence is admissible in court in the US (except for Nebraska apparently).[20] The kind of respect one gives the Bloodhound is the sort that is given truly out of a sense of admiration. That's the kind of respect that is long-lasting and is not tied to punitive measures. That is indeed the kind of respect leaders should be striving for—why bother being respected because people are scared of you? Wouldn't it be so much neater to be respected because of your positive and amiable qualities? One can showcase one's capabilities without being a fearsome individual.

I remember this old Bloodhound named Billy, who belonged to a friend of mine (Molly Cisco, who sadly passed away some years ago). Billy was a big hound, but what a perfect gentleman or gentle-hound, he was. He had an independent streak about him, which you could see working when he'd catch a scent, and he'd take off. But he would be ever so polite in all matters—you could tell that he was a dog of refined breeding. You'd never be scared or fearful of him, but you'd know that that was a dog worthy of being respected, and he'd be respectful himself too. That's the sort of respect we should all be

60 LEARNING LEADERSHIP FROM DOGS

aiming for—the genial kind of respect that sustains itself and stays lit like an eternal flame.

I'd like to discuss a dog breed here that I'm fairly sure few people will know of, well unless they happen to be real dog aficionados or French. I am referring to the Grand Bleu de Gascogne,[21] which is such a strikingly beautiful dog. This breed is referred to as the King of Hounds, for its elegant and striking appearance. The color pattern of the Grand Bleu de Gascogne is black on white, with blue. Unfortunately, the dog is practically unknown in the US—as far as I know, there was only one breeder, and that breeder stopped breeding the dog, because of lack of interest from people. I remember that breeder lamenting that it was a pity such a beautiful dog didn't make it big in America. An anecdote from the past mentions that George Washington had seven Grand Bleu de Gascogne hounds, which he used for hunting.

Apparently, the Grand Bleu's were unable to hunt raccoons because raccoons could climb trees—this led to the eventual creation of Coonhounds (who will make their appearance in Chapter 11), who were able to hunt Raccoons a lot better than the Grand Bleu de Gascogne hounds were. But regardless of the dog's popularity in the US, it continues to be a well-respected and dignified hound back in France. The respect that is accorded to the Grand Bleu de Gascogne is the kind of respect that is sustainable and a mix of capability and demeanor.

Another dog breed that really embodies this be respectful receive respectful theme is the Borzoi or the Russian Wolfhound.[22,23] These are tall elegant and dignified dogs—they were kept by Russian Royalty and even the Tsars. Sadly, after the Russian Revolution, many Borzois were killed because they were a symbol of aristocracy. Luckily, due to the efforts of a soldier named Constantin Esmont, the government was convinced to help preserve the breed as it was useful for hunters. And of course, Borzoi fanciers from the UK and US also helped in the preservation of this beautiful regal breed. These are tall dogs and excellent sighthounds.

Rather similar but slighter than the Irish Wolfhounds discussed in Chapter 5. Again, this polite and regal hound obtains respect just by dint of its wonderfully kind nature as well as its exemplary hunting skills. We should all feel very fortunate that we didn't lose the Borzoi as another casualty of the Russian Revolution.

Speaking of revolutions, another famous revolution (if not the most famous one) is the French Revolution. That event could have torpedoed another breed (the low-slung Basset Hound), but surprisingly while the immediate aftermath did see many Bassets losing their lives, eventually the dog became popular as a common man's dog and was used as an excellent hunter of rabbits and hare. The Basset Hound[24] is pretty heavy weight-wise compared with its fairly low-to-the-ground height. This is yet another dog breed that you simply cannot help but respect—it might have to do with its solemn expressions or its flawless sense of smell. Bassets also tend to be superb themselves in the politeness aspects of demeanor. I remember a Basset I knew named Buffy, who belonged to a really dear-to-me family (The Claytons, Ed, Pat, and Zach). Buffy was a wonderful and such a lovely respectful dog. Most Basset Hounds are like that—they may look like low-slung dogs, but their solemn appearance cannot but fail to catapult them into the ranks of the respected. Now I'm finally going to discuss a breed that is especially near and dear to my heart—indeed, one could suggest that it is probably one of the closest to my ground [...]. I mean heart. I refer to the brilliant and spiffing Dachshund.

Now I'm sure people reading this book, at least, the ones who've never had the privilege of having a Dachshund in their households, may be furrowing their brows in puzzlement to see the Dachshund in this list. But Dachshund owners at this point are probably smiling knowing yet wry smiles. You see despite its size, the Dachshund has a real booming bark, and if you don't see a Dachshund barking, you might end up thinking that's the bark of a significantly larger dog. I know my Buddy (a lovely smooth Red Dachshund) had such a sonorous bark, that people often thought he was a German Shepherd or some other larger breed, till they saw him in person.

Buddy was an awesome dog, and I really miss him. He lived to a glorious fourteen and a half years and retained his booming bark till the end. Except for the one time when he got a sore throat and didn't bark at all one day. That got my dad really worried, and he took him to the vet urgently, and after that, it was a bit of an anticlimax when the vet revealed that Buddy had a sore throat after possibly barking too much the previous day.

The Dachshund is a German breed,[25] which was developed to hunt badgers, and as most people probably know by now, the Badger is not an animal that is shy using its sharp teeth and claws. Dachshunds had to often times go underground into tunnels in their pursuit of their larger quarry, and part of the reason, why they have such booming barks. The barks needed to be loud for the human hunters who were still above ground, and so able to figure out where the Dachshunds were underneath. The Dachshund comes in a variety of sizes, colors, and coats, including red and black and tan, as well as smooth coated, or wirehaired, or longhaired. While all Dachshunds do have common characteristics, there are certain subtle differences between the trio. The longhaired and the wire-haired ones tend to be a bit more laidback than the smooth ones, but I'd say that the longhaired and smooth

62   LEARNING LEADERSHIP FROM DOGS

varieties are probably the most popular types in the Dachshund world. Now the Dachshund not only deserves respect but also ensures that others know it deserves respect.

The Dachshund is one of the most intelligent and boldly vigilant dogs out there and is one of the best watchdogs of all. The principle we should all learn from Dachshunds is that sometimes it becomes necessary to demand that others respect you. This can be done by your showing up and performing or excelling in a certain domain, or it could be simply done by your bringing that to the attention of the concerned party. Take a look at LinkedIn, where all and sundry are busy self-promoting themselves incessantly—okay, maybe that's a bad example. But take a little bit of that sentiment and dial it down a notch, and you have the Dachshund approach right down pat. Be assertive and not overly dominant, and you have the right approach to being respectful about demanding respect. Now, let's tie all this information and relay it back to how leaders can use this information.

What Do Leaders Need to Take from This?

Now I've gone and discussed several breeds of dogs in this particular chapter—might well be the most I've done in any chapter thus far. What can we learn from all of these various dogs, and indeed, the various shades of respect? I would say that we can learn a little bit from every shade of respect. Right off the bat, it is important to be skilled and competent in your job duties—every dog which has been discussed in this chapter is excellent and highly skilled in their purpose. Fila Brasileiros, for instance, are second to none when it comes to guarding large estates, and likewise, Borzois are unbeatable by most other dogs when it comes to coursing prey. Consider that a hypothetical leader who is incompetent in his or her domain of work is unlikely to generate much respect, regardless of whether or not he or she is an amiable person. So, for any leader, who hopes to be respected by his or her followers or others, the first step is to ensure that that leader truly has competence in the area they're leading in. The ones who get into a leadership position and lack any competence, and also lack any initiative to gain competence or skills will never be able to generate any sort of respect toward themselves.

The next step is to be respectful of yourself. Imitate the Bloodhound or the Grand Bleu de Gascogne, and be amiable, polite, and respectful to others. If this is combined with a modicum of competence, then there's nothing to beat that. It may sound like simplistic guru-like dialogue to say be respectful and be worthy of respect, but it's absolutely true. You have to give respect and be capable of generating respect from others. And of course, if you find yourself not getting any respect back, then perhaps take a cue from the Dachshund, and vociferously demand that you be accorded respect, which is due to you. And yes, there is also the fact that you could demand respect from others by relying on their being fearful of you, similar to the Fila Brasileiro or the Dogo Argentino, but I wouldn't rely on the fear factor all that much. It's not sustainable, and the respect generated by that may not be genuine either. So, in short, leaders need to create and improve their own capabilities and make their competence and skills known to all. If a leader just skulks in their office without being out there, even if they're supremely capable, nobody else will know that, and as a result, there's not going to be a whole lot of respect generated.

Summary

In this chapter, I discuss the concept of respect and outline why it is important for leaders to not only be respectful but also to be respected in return. One cannot be only one and ignore the other requirement. I have discussed dog breeds like the Mastiff, Rottweiler, Dogo Argentino, Basset Hound, Dachshund, among others in the context of respect. In Chapter 7, I will be diving into the topic of gratitude and describe and discuss certain dog breeds that exemplify the quality of gratitude.

Dobermann Pinscher

Mastiff

Rottweiler

Neapolitan Mastiff

Borzoi

Grand Bleu de Gascogne   Dachshund

Presa Canario

Japanese Tosa

Fila Brasileiro   Dogo Argentino

Bloodhound

Basset Hound

Cane Corso

References

1 Vasconcelos, A. F. (2020). Workplace incivility: A literature review. *International Journal of Workplace Health Management*, 13(5), 513–542.
2 Young, K. A., Hassan, S., & Hatmaker, D. M. (2021). Towards understanding workplace incivility: Gender, ethical leadership and personal control. *Public Management Review*, 23(1), 31–52.
3 Loh, J. M., Thorsteinsson, E. B., & Loi, N. M. (2021). Workplace incivility and work outcomes: Cross-cultural comparison between Australian and Singaporean employees. *Asia Pacific Journal of Human Resources*, 59(2), 305–329.
4 https://www.akc.org/dog-breeds/rottweiler/.
5 https://www.thekennelclub.org.uk/search/breeds-a-to-z/breeds/working/rottweiler/.
6 https://www.akc.org/dog-breeds/doberman-pinscher/.
7 https://www.thekennelclub.org.uk/search/breeds-a-to-z/breeds/working/dobermann/.
8 https://www.akc.org/dog-breeds/mastiff/.
9 https://www.thekennelclub.org.uk/search/breeds-a-to-z/breeds/working/mastiff/.
10 https://www.akc.org/dog-breeds/neapolitan-mastiff/.
11 https://www.thekennelclub.org.uk/search/breeds-a-to-z/breeds/working/neapolitan-mastiff/.
12 https://ckcusa.com/breeds/fila-brasileiro/.
13 https://www.akc.org/expert-advice/dog-breeds/how-does-a-dog-breed-become-akc-recognized/.

66 LEARNING LEADERSHIP FROM DOGS

14 https://www.akc.org/dog-breeds/tosa/.
15 https://www.akc.org/dog-breeds/dogo-argentino/.
16 https://www.akc.org/dog-breeds/presa-canario/.
17 https://www.akc.org/dog-breeds/cane-corso/.
18 https://www.thekennelclub.org.uk/search/breeds-a-to-z/breeds/hound/bloodhound/.
19 https://www.akc.org/dog-breeds/bloodhound/.
20 https://www.courthousenews.com/dogs-for-the-prosecution/.
21 https://www.thekennelclub.org.uk/search/breeds-a-to-z/breeds/hound/grand-bleu-de-gascogne-imp/.
22 https://www.thekennelclub.org.uk/search/breeds-a-to-z/breeds/hound/borzoi/.
23 https://www.akc.org/dog-breeds/borzoi/.
24 https://www.akc.org/dog-breeds/basset-hound/.
25 https://www.thekennelclub.org.uk/search/breeds-a-to-z/breeds/hound/dachshund-smooth-haired/.

Chapter 7

GREAT/ER (DANE OR SWISS) GRATITUDE

Gratitude is a quality that I personally consider to be a fundamental one, in terms of how a person's character can be measured. After all, as social creatures of this world, a bit of gratitude goes a long way, in ensuring that the fabric of community and togetherness continues on for the foreseeable future. However, as so many recent and past events have demonstrated to us, gratitude is a quality that seems to be singularly lacking in a lot of people. We've all probably had an unsavory encounter or two with someone who displayed zero gratitude to us, even when we did that person a favor. And then there are times when the ingratitude really reeks.

Think about the example of the one CEO who fired her employee, after the employee even donated her kidney to the boss.[1,2] Just typing that sentence out makes me squirm uncomfortably—can you even imagine what sort of heartless (unfortunately, no longer kidney less thanks to the generous act by the ex-employee) human being that boss must be? Zero gratitude can be detected there, which is such a sad statement to be writing about. If someone does you a favor or pulls some strings for you, then the decent thing to do is to at least feel a bit of gratitude for that person. But sadly, far too many people exist who simply cannot fathom that simple fact—yes, sure, there are times when one may need to withhold said gratitude, depending on what is being asked of one. For instance, if someone is expecting you to engage in a crime or unethical action, then maybe, doing that out of gratitude isn't such a great idea (unless one fancies a resultant tense interview with a judicial representative and a long stint in prison).

For me, gratitude is a quality that no other living being shows quite as well as do dogs. I suppose, cats and birds do that on occasion, but dogs are the Kings and Queens of embodying gratitude. Anyone who's ever given a treat to any dog will attest to this—watch the sparkling eyes, and the steadily increasing tempo of the wagging tail, and you can get a measure of how grateful that dog is, for a simple treat or a kind word. I would wager that dogs are eons ahead of humans when it comes to embodying gratitude; however,

68   LEARNING LEADERSHIP FROM DOGS

that does mean that we can learn loads from dogs about how to better express and react with gratitude to kindness or concern displayed by others. As is the custom in this book, I will discuss several breeds of dogs, who I believe are fabulous examples of exemplifying gratitude.

In this chapter, I will center my explanation and discussion on how one can channel a sense of gratitude, and also how one can inspire others to display some gratitude themselves. Just like the other qualities previously discussed, having a sense of gratitude is important, but it's also important to work with individuals and people who display and embody gratitude themselves. One of the common themes I think should reflect throughout the book is that no quality should be taken to the extreme, even gratitude. You do not need to overdo it, especially if demonstrating gratitude ends up causing people to engage in unethical activities.

As always, the chapter will feature a plethora of dog breeds, which can teach us about to exemplify gratitude and show the way forward for our associates to engage with and display gratitude too. I will start off by discussing some dogs, who we should truly be grateful for. These are dogs that have helped so many humans across the globe in a variety of tasks, and those are tasks that simply could not have been accomplished without these dogs. Let's start off, shall we.

Dogs that We Should Be Super Grateful for [...] And Learn about Gratitude to Boot

Now of course, we ought to be grateful for all varieties of dogs, but in this section, I'm going to focus on some specialty breeds, which really emphasize the need for gratitude from us for their existence. Let's start off with the Swiss Mountain Dogs, shall we? This is a super popular dog breed and a splendidly happy dog at that. The Bernese Mountain Dog[3,4] is another super kind breed out there, and incredibly puppyish for a long while. If you get a Bernese Mountain Dog, you are basically getting a big puppy for a long time. Sadly, the Bernese Mountain Dog's typical lifespan is quite low (lesser than 10 years), which is somewhat of a norm in many large breeds. As its name suggests, the dog originates from the Swiss canton of Berne and was originally used as a farm dog, and especially used to pull carts containing cheese and milk to market. This is a super affectionate dog and thrives on company. It would be unusually cruel to leave a Bernese Mountain Dog alone away from family, especially today when the dog is a family dog and not a working dog. The Berners (a nickname of the breed) are also amazing therapy dogs for people across generations (i.e., the elderly and children). If you've never met a Berner before, you've really missed out—the Bernese Mountain Dog is an

GREAT/ER (DANE OR SWISS) GRATITUDE   69

amazing and beautiful dog, that one has to feel grateful for. Their delightful expressions apart and their comical yet reliable temperaments make them simply astounding as family dogs. Check out the multitude of videos of Berners with kids—you can literally see the happiness in both the kids and the dogs. And Bernese Mountain Dogs are second to none when it comes to displaying gratitude to their owners. They love to make and keep their owners and family members happy, and this sort of organic gratitude they display is heart-warming to the hilt. It's also super fun to run into a Berner at the dog park—this one time, a Bernese Mountain Dog named Brenner saw me and my two kids in a dog park. The entire duration that day, he hung out with us, just because one of my kids offered him a treat. Gratitude of a sort, rarely if ever seen in humans, isn't it?

Another breed which is related to the Bernese Mountain Dog is the Greater Swiss Mountain Dog.[5] It has a similar coat color as the Berners do, but their coats tend to be short as opposed to the Bernese's double coats, and the Greater Swiss' bodies tend to be slightly less plump. They also don't get along with every single entity out there unlike the more amiable Bernese Mountain Dogs, but regardless, the Greater Swiss Mountain Dogs also seem to possess a wonderful and innate sense of gratitude. To see the sight of a Greater Swiss pulling a cart and still managing to look majestic is quite a wholesome one. One of my neighbors had a Greater Swiss Mountain Dog, who you could visibly see always gazing at the neighbor. Sure, most dogs do gaze at their owners, and there are plenty of recent studies which explore why dogs do that, and it appears that the consensus is that dogs do so in order to gauge their owner's emotions.[6,7] But the look that the Greater Swiss Mountain Dog gave his owner was a picture-perfect depiction of gratitude, and I really wish I had taken a picture at the time to be able to reproduce here. But let me also talk about another "Great" breed—yes, the universally renowned Great Dane.[8,9]

A large part of the fame that Great Danes have is due to the universal popularity of the Scooby Doo character from the cartoon series. However, unlike Scooby Doo, these dogs are not necessarily cowardly dogs, but they are absolutely adoringly gentle. They are large enough that burglars or wrongdoers unaware of the true nature of Great Danes will be scared off of their attempted misdemeanor. The Great Danes are giant breeds, rivaling the Irish Wolfhound, although the Wolfhound does tend to be slightly taller. Great Danes exhibit fantastic stature, and are indeed, sometimes called the Apollo of Dogs. And despite their name, the Great Dane originally hails from Germany. In fact, the Great Dane is the national dog of Germany—I must say when I first learned that fact, I was really amazed, as I'd always thought that the national dog was either the German Shepherd or the Dachshund,

70   LEARNING LEADERSHIP FROM DOGS

but it turned out to be the Great Dane. I suppose the Germans probably wanted to make sure Denmark didn't quietly usurp their dog. To look upon the majestic countenance of the Great Dane is to immediately feel a sense of awe that will permeate your entire being.

The Great Danes of yore were essentially used as Boar Hounds (remember the fact about Hagrid's Fang from Chapter 6?) The original German Boarhounds were a mixture of mastiffs and Irish Wolfhounds, which were then bred with Greyhounds, and that resulted in the Great Dane we know today. These dogs can weigh up to 120 pounds, but it's their height that is so remarkable—they can get as tall as 30 inches. They are also a giant breed that can easily be kept as house pets, of course, provided the house isn't too cramped. They do need some space to loll around the house. These dogs again are just fantastic in the gratitude department—they are naturally friendly toward people and other animals. And they will repay your kindness to them manifold. Now that I sort of snuck a little bit of persiflage at Denmark in my previous paragraph, let me make amends by talking about a Danish breed of dog.

This is a relatively unknown breed, at least out of its native country of Denmark. I first happened to learn about the breed about a decade ago, when I was interested in learning about the various mastiffs of the world. And lo and behold—there was the Danish Mastiff aka the Broholmer.[10] It also turned out that there was a Broholmer breeder right in Wisconsin, in Appleton, to be precise. After that, I did a lot more reading and digging into information about the Broholmer and even got to meet a Broholmer at one point. This is another breed that is a perfect example of how to embody gratitude. Unlike its past purpose as a "Butcher's Dog," today's Broholmer is pretty much happy and content to be a family pet. The Broholmer's imposing size will serve to keep unsavory intruders at bay, but again, people in the know will know that the Broholmer is a super kind and friendly breed, who loves to snuggle (as per many Broholmer owners) with their families. Several Broholmer owners I have corresponded with tell me that their Broholmers are especially expressive with their gratitude.

Now there is one reason why many folks probably don't know a whole lot about Broholmers unless they're real dog aficionados or have connections with Denmark. The reason is that the Broholmer was almost extinct after World War II, and it took the efforts of a group called The Society for Reconstruction of the Broholmer Breed (a rather neat society name). So anyhow, I suppose we must also express gratitude to these breed proponents, who have helped save so many magnificent breeds from becoming extinct.

Before diving into more discussion of specific dog breeds, it is important to take a step back and discuss gratitude itself. Now there are several forms of gratitude—one form involves the affective or trait-based form of gratitude,

GREAT/ER (DANE OR SWISS) GRATITUDE   71

while the other two involve feelings and emotion-based gratitude.[11-13] The latter two forms of gratitude are much more ephemeral than the first one, which basically means that the gratitude that results from one's mood or one's emotion is likely to be transient. The kind of gratitude that I believe we can learn from dogs is the trait-based form of gratitude. Dogs are intrinsically grateful beings and exhibit their gratitude toward us in a variety of ways. It is important that we see and acknowledge that gratitude, and in turn, manifest it ourselves. Express gratitude and recognize gratitude—both are important.

Alright, Now Back to Dogs Again

The next breed I'm going to discuss has become rather legendary in terms of being associated with gratitude. I refer to the Akita,[14] a strong powerful Japanese breed of dog. The Akita I am referring to as legendary is Hachi-ko,[15] who was a dog owned by Professor Ueno in Tokyo. Hachi-ko would accompany the Professor to Shibuya Station when the Professor would go there to catch a train to go to work. Hachi-ko would then wait for him the whole day so as to be able to walk back with him. One day, the Professor died at work and never did make it back. Hachi-ko waited for him for over ten years, and in the process, became a Japanese national hero for his unwavering loyalty, which was borne out of his gratitude for Professor Ueno's love for him.

The Akita now has a distinct American variety called the Akita, while the Japanese variety is called the Akita-Inu. This discussion will feature both varieties here because apart from the American variety being significantly larger, both dog breeds have similar traits and dignified expressions. Although, I must say that at least the American variety of the Akita seems to be somewhat domineering with other dog breeds—they're great with their own human families, but a bit overprotective when other dogs are concerned. Every time, I've seen an Akita while walking around with mine, the Akita's owners are always hesitant to let their dogs meet mine or anyone else's dog for that matter. I guess, maybe they had experiences where their Akita was a bit unfriendly toward the other dog. It's just a trait of the Akita that's carried over through the ages, since in its early form, it was intended to be a fighting breed. The Akita happens to be the national dog of Japan and symbolizes good luck. You can buy Akita symbol chains and magnets, and it's supposed to help usher in good luck for you. Of course, getting an Akita as a pet will probably bring in good luck for you as well, since they are super loving toward their own family.

Another breed which I simply have to mention here in connection with gratitude is the Siberian Husky.[16] The Husky is also a really popular mascot which several universities in the US have adopted—this list includes universities in Maine, Washington, Connecticut, Illinois, and Massachusetts.

72   LEARNING LEADERSHIP FROM DOGS

So, one reason why I think here we need to be expressing gratitude to the Husky is because of one brave Husky in the past named Balto. The Husky in the discussion was a sled dog originally bred for dogsled racing. In 1925, there was an urgent need for a diphtheria vaccine in Nome, Alaska. But there was a harsh raging blizzard, and a freezing river, in the way. Balto and his team braved the blizzard and the freezing river and got the much-needed vaccine to Nome from Anchorage. This of course helped prevent an otherwise inevitable epidemic, and Balto basically got immortalized in our memories. There are probably numerous people across Alaska who owe their very existence to Balto (i.e., the many descendants of the people saved from passing away thanks to the prompt delivery of the precious vaccine).

The Siberian Husky has been associated with the Chukchi people in Siberia, and as the name signals, needs to have both endurance and a disposition to work. Huskies also have incredibly thick double coats and bushy tails to keep warm. These are peaceful and lovable companion dogs, who get along with people and other dogs. Most sled dogs tend to be amiable breeds, and the Husky is no different. Of course, this amiability makes the Husky a fairly futile guard dog, but in any event, if someone wants a guard dog, there are other dogs to be gotten. The Husky is a different kind of animal altogether, and does tend to be independent minded and need lots and lots of exercise. It is also not uncommon for Huskies to love hanging out in the snow during the winter months. So, if concerned neighbors get worried at seeing a Husky hanging out in the cold freezing winter snow, they should realize that it's a Husky in question, and not an Italian Greyhound or a Peruvian Hairless. For the latter dogs, absolutely, call the authorities or your neighbors to tell them to let their dogs in. But cold weather has never fazed a Siberian Husky. Not just the Chukchi people, but really, anyone who has ever used Huskies to help them in polar or Arctic expeditions or dogsled operations, owes a modicum of gratitude for Siberian Huskies. Next, I will discuss a "huskier" distant cousin of the Siberian Husky, namely the Alaskan Malamute.[17]

There is no confusing a Husky with an Alaskan Malamute—if anything, the Malamutes tend to be far "huskier" in appearance than the Huskies. They are significantly larger and heavier-built dogs, even if they do look a bit similar. The Malamutes are named after the Inuit tribe called the Mahlemiut, who hail from Alaska. The Alaskan Malamutes were used as sled dogs and a good imagery to use to compare them with their distant Husky cousins is to think of the Malamutes as a sturdy truck that goes long distances carrying heavy loads at low speeds, while the Huskies are more like nifty sport cars that go shorter distances carrying lighter loads at high speed.

There is a great deal of gratitude we and our forebears owe to the Alaskan Malamutes—these Malamute breeds were used by the Gold Rush of 1896

GREAT/ER (DANE OR SWISS) GRATITUDE 73

in Alaska by prospectors.[18] It is no exaggeration to claim that many of those prospectors would have died miserable deaths without their Malamutes, who were indispensable in terms of helping them by being pack dogs for carrying food and supplies. I've met this pair of Malamutes in a nearby dog park, and they are almost twice as big as a normal Husky. The male Malamute is also a bit uncertain around other male dogs, so I'm not sure the Malamute owner should be bringing his dogs to dog parks. Alaskan Malamute males do tend to be a bit aggressive with other dogs, so that's another difference with Huskies, who are chilled-out dogs with every other breed out there. But regardless, we should be grateful to the Alaskan Malamute for being such a wonderful and helpful dog breed—Admiral Richard Byrd could have hardly explored so much of Antarctica without Malamutes in his team and on his side. And in Alaska, up until the 1960s, sled dogs consisting of Malamutes were used to deliver mail reliably. Probably more environmentally friendly as well, come to think of it!

Passing on from the frozen Tundra, let us pass into the cloudy skies of Ireland to discuss a dog breed, whose origins are a lot more proletarian than royal. The dog in question is the pleasing Wheaten Terrier, also called the Irish Poor Man's dog.[19,20] There used to be an old British law called "The Laws of the Forest" which prevented non-land-owning people from owning hunting dogs like Hounds or Spaniels. Additionally, the law prevented non-land-owning folks from hunting or sporting dogs who were taller than 19 inches or had long tails.

Quite a lot of ridiculous prohibitions, if one judges from today's era, but at that time, that is, more than 200 years ago, they were seen as being rightful and just. Passing along from unjust laws like that, we can now turn to the Wheaten Terrier. This dog breed turned out to be supremely versatile and could accomplish a variety of tasks. The landless among the Irish could still have a dog and what a dog the Wheaten Terrier was and is. This is one of the most versatile breeds out there and is keen to work and willing to work regardless of the weather. Sometimes the Wheaten Terrier is also called the poor man's Irish Wolfhound, and its height almost comes close to that limit which the "Laws of the Forest" established; however, the Wheatens do come with tails docked, and that tradition has persisted through the ages. That was supposed to avoid taxes for owning dogs with full plumy tails.

The Wheaten Terrier is a playful and friendly dog, although it can become excessively verbose (i.e., barks a bunch) if bored. Today, of course, anyone can keep dogs, and there are few dogs that are only reserved for royal family members, but the origins of the Wheaten Terrier, and its excellent usefulness for folks, even if they weren't of royal or landowning status makes you understand how much gratitude one ought to feel for a Wheaten Terrier. And these dogs are beautiful—I've seen and met a couple of them, and they totally lived up to their reputation as masterful "Wheaten Greeting" experts.

74 LEARNING LEADERSHIP FROM DOGS

The "Wheaten Greeting" refers to the bouncy jump Wheaten Terriers give when meeting people or greeting adored ones.

Sticking to the Terrier motif, I must also mention a Terrier, which has become increasingly rare in modern times but is famous for being a dog breed that was named after a character in a famous piece of literature. I am of course speaking of the Dandie Dinmont Terrier, which is an adorable rough coated small Terrier, who was named after a character (Dandie Dinmont) from the novel Guy Mannering written by Sir Walter Scott. This is the only AKC-recognized breed that was named after a fictional character. Isn't that something? I'm sure in the years to come, with all of the new designer dog combos coming in the market, we will eventually end up with Clark Kent Hounds and Bruce Wayne Pinschers, but as of now, the Dandies are the only breed with that recognition. This is a beautiful breed, but increasingly rare now.[21] I have never met a Dandie Dinmont Terrier in person yet, but hope to finally meet one when I next travel to California, as there is a Dandie Dinmont breeder there. It would be awesome to finally meet some members of this historically significant dog breed. I've read plenty about Dandie Dinmonts, but it would be nice to actually get to meet one in person.

From all descriptions, it appears that the Dandie Dinmont Terrier is yet another "big little dog," which usually means that they are not a dainty little dog, as their name might suggest. In the old days, they were used to hunt badgers and otters, and they have a deep bark, not unlike another badger hunter, the Dachshund. Unlike some smaller dogs, Dandies love playing with children, so they are a great breed to keep as a family pet. Like all Terriers though, they can be somewhat independent minded and stubborn, so a bit of patience is handy. The breed has been around since the 1700s, and it is rather unfortunate that it's now become a rare breed—one cannot help but feel gratitude for the extant members of this breed. Now I'm going to talk about some ways by which we can increase our own sense of gratitude.

Trick or 'Tude

All of the previous contents in the book focused on several breeds of dogs, who can help arouse a sense of gratitude in us. Now I'm going to discuss some methods by which we can increase our own trait gratitude levels. I mean it's one thing to tell someone to express or experience gratitude, it's quite another to give them the tools to do so. One of the best methods by which one can improve one's sense of gratitude is to basically keep a gratitude diary or journal. A plethora of research has demonstrated that gratitude diaries have positive effects on a whole host of people[22,23]— they work wonders for distressed individuals, both adults and children.

GREAT/ER (DANE OR SWISS) GRATITUDE

Maintaining a gratitude journal can help increase a person's sense of wellbeing, and those effects can be long-lasting. A meta-analysis found that gratitude in particular can influence happiness, which is certainly an outcome most people would wish for.

Another trick which really does wonders in increasing trait gratitude is to practice meditation.[24,25] This can be tricky, of course—one does need a sense of relative tranquil prior to attempting to meditate. Full disclaimer here—I personally struggle with meditating especially when there's a lot going on in my life. All the thoughts keep swirling around, and it gets a bit difficult to truly meditate. But many people I know do this, and it works really well for them—this includes my spouse who makes it a point to meditate on a daily basis.

Yet, another tool to help increase trait gratitude is to reframe negative situations into positive situations. This can be done decently by most individuals, although it may take some practice prior to doing it successfully. To reframe a situation is to basically examine the situation without getting overwhelmed by the situation. An example of it is as follows—let's say you failed an exam. While that can be disheartening, it's not the end of the world. Most exams can be retaken, and failures don't need to keep repeating. So, one way to incorporate gratitude here is to tell yourself that even though you failed the exam, you still learned from it, and are grateful to be able to reattempt the exam. With an attitude like that, the next attempted exam is bound to go better.

From a leadership perspective, it is important to only demonstrate that you have a sense of gratitude because your showing will help your followers gain a sense of gratitude as well. Gratitude and its links with subjective well-being and happiness make it apparent that it is a quality that should be encouraged in and by leaders, not just for the leader's sake but for the follower's sake too. There are many other ways by which you can improve your overall sense of gratitude or trait of gratitude, but the three mentioned above are quite possibly the best ones. When it comes to dogs, we owe them loads of gratitude, and by watching and observing how much gratitude they espouse themselves, we can certainly improve our own sense of gratitude.

Summary

In this chapter, I discuss the concept of gratitude and outline why it is important for individuals to have gratitude. I have discussed dog breeds like the Great Dane, Siberian Husky, Alaskan Malamute, Wheaten Terrier, among others in the context of gratitude. I have also briefly discussed three ways by which we can improve our own sense of gratitude. In Chapter 8, I will be discussing the topic of trust, and discuss and describe several dog breeds that exemplify the quality of trust.

Great Dane

Greater Swiss Mountain Dog

Bernese Mountain Dog

Akita

Broholmer

Soft Coated Wheaten Terrier

Alaskan Malamute

Dandie Dinmont Terrier

Siberian Husky

References

1 https://www.reuters.com/article/idUSBRE83N1G1/.
2 https://abcnews.go.com/News/york-mom-fired-donating-kidney-boss/story?id= 16195691.
3 https://www.akc.org/dog-breeds/bernese-mountain-dog/.
4 https://www.thekennelclub.org.uk/search/breeds-a-to-z/breeds/working/bernese-mountain-dog/.
5 https://www.thekennelclub.org.uk/search/breeds-a-to-z/breeds/working/great-swiss-mountain-dog/.
6 Koyasu, H., Kikusui, T., Takagi, S., & Nagasawa, M. (2020). The gaze communications between dogs/cats and humans: Recent research review and future directions. *Frontiers in Psychology*, 11, 613512.
7 Hoel, J. A., Templeton, G. B., Fefer, G., Case, B. C., Shah, A., Gruen, M. E., & Olby, N. J. (2021). Sustained gaze is a reliable in-home test of attention for aging pet dogs. *Frontiers in Veterinary Science*, 8, 819135.
8 https://www.akc.org/dog-breeds/great-dane/.
9 https://www.thekennelclub.org.uk/search/breeds-a-to-z/breeds/working/great-dane/.
10 https://www.akc.org/dog-breeds/broholmer/.
11 Shin, L. J., Armenta, C. N., Kamble, S. V., Chang, S. L., Wu, H. Y., & Lyubomirsky, S. (2020). Gratitude in collectivist and individualist cultures. *The Journal of Positive Psychology*, 15(5), 598–604.
12 Kong, F., Yang, K., Yan, W., & Li, X. (2021). How does trait gratitude relate to subjective well- being in Chinese adolescents? The mediating role of resilience and social support. *Journal of Happiness Studies*, 22, 1611–1622.
13 Boggio, P. S., Giglio, A. C. A., Nakao, C. K., Wingenbach, T. S. H., Marques, L. M., Koller, S., & Gruber, J. (2020). Writing about gratitude increases emotion-regulation efficacy. *The Journal of Positive Psychology*, 15(6), 783–794.
14 https://www.akc.org/dog-breeds/akita/.
15 https://vickiandhachi.com/the-truth-about-hachiko-the-loyal-akita/.
16 https://www.akc.org/dog-breeds/siberian-husky/.
17 https://www.akc.org/dog-breeds/alaskan-malamute/.
18 https://lifeinnotions.com/alaskan-arctic-expedition-with-alaskan-malamutes/.
19 https://www.akc.org/dog-breeds/soft-coated-wheaten-terrier/.
20 https://www.akc.org/expert-advice/dog-breeds/soft-coated-wheaten-terrier-history-ireland/.
21 https://www.thekennelclub.org.uk/search/breeds-a-to-z/breeds/terrier/dandie-dinmont-terrier/.
22 Boggiss, A. L., Consedine, N. S., Brenton-Peters, J. M., Hofman, P. L., & Serlachius, A. S. (2020). A systematic review of gratitude interventions: Effects on physical health and health behaviors. *Journal of Psychosomatic Research*, 135, 110165.
23 Jiang, D. (2022). Feeling gratitude is associated with better well-being across the life span: A daily diary study during the COVID-19 outbreak. *The Journals of Gerontology: Series B*, 77(4), e36–e45.
24 Fraser, E., Misener, K., & Libben, M. (2022). Exploring the impact of a gratitude-focused meditation on body dissatisfaction: Can a brief auditory gratitude intervention protect young women against exposure to the thin ideal? *Body Image*, 41, 331–341.
25 Strohmaier, S., Jones, F. W., & Cane, J. E. (2022). One-session mindfulness of the breath meditation practice: A randomized controlled study of the effects on state hope and state gratitude in the general population. *Mindfulness*, 13, 162–173.

Chapter 8

TERRIER'IZING TRUST

This topic was slated for an earlier placement in the book, but then while writing the book, I figured that a previous chapter made more sense to be moved up, so it became prudent to move trust down to this chapter instead. Trust is another quality that is integrally tied to effective leadership. The whole point of leadership is to be able to influence followers, and in optimal cases, be able to influence them without coercion. You have to get them to follow you despite any rewards or punishments—the key to doing that is Trust. When followers trust their leaders, they are more willing to stick up for and support their leader's plans and visions.[1-4] And ditto for leaders—if they trust their followers, they are more likely to listen to their followers and more likely to practice an empowering style of leadership with them as opposed to the dreary and dread-inducing micromanagement style of leading.[5,6] which needless to say signals a lack of trust on the leader's behalf, and also ensures that the followers never trust their leader either.

In this chapter, I will focus on the concept of trust, and discuss how important and essential it is in establishing effective leadership. Without trust, one may as well take one's ball home and call it a day. Trust is integral in helping people follow and adhere to a vision set by the leader. There is a plethora of ways by which leaders can help their followers trust them, and I will discuss some of those behaviors in this particular chapter. When it comes to followers, it is important for leaders to trust them as well. It is absolutely suboptimal to have situations or conditions where only followers trust their leaders, but the leaders don't reciprocate the trust back.

Dogs are synonymous with trust—after all, the old saying about a person's best friend being his or her dog exists for a reason. Another human being may betray your trust over trivial or nontrivial matters, but a dog will never do that. Humans trust their dogs for a reason, and dogs too trust their humans (although sadly, in some cases, the trust is misplaced, and many of those humans aren't worthy of that level of trust). But if the humans in question are indeed worthy of that loyalty, then it's pure perfection. In this chapter, like every other one before it, and every other one ahead of it, I will discuss a variety of dog breeds that exemplify trust. I will also discuss ways by which we can improve our own

80   LEARNING LEADERSHIP FROM DOGS

abilities to engender trust and to (yes!) trust others. It is important to learn to trust others—living life while being distrustful of every person out there is hardly a good life to lead, and can be quite stressful, in actuality. Being constantly distrustful of others can lead one to become paranoid, which is never a good state of being to be in. Alright, on to dogs now—the title of this chapter took a bit of a turn because I had initially intended to name it Tosa Bone for Trust, but then since I've already introduced the Tosa in a previous chapter, I decided to name the chapter "Terrier'izing Trust" instead, as I thought to focus a lot of space on the various Terrier types in this chapter. Upon scrutiny of the various breeds covered so far, it felt like Terriers were getting a bit underrepresented. So, to counter the imbalance, I'm going to discuss plenty of Terriers in this chapter.

Trust Us

I already discussed the Wheaten Terrier and the Dandie Dinmont Terrier in Chapter 7, so let's go with a Terrier, which I think will be an interesting unique one for most readers—I refer of course to the Kerry Blue Terrier.[7] This strikingly handsome dog is from Ireland, and as the name suggests, hails from the county of Kerry in Ireland. The Blue in the name refers to the fact that these dogs have bluish-gray coats—they're not blue like one expects the Smurfs or Sonic the Hedgehog to be, but they are sort of bluish in color. So, anyhow, the Kerry Blue Terrier is a breed that has a fantastic backstory (apocryphal as it may well be). Really fantastic, quite the stuff of legends! So, let's hear the legend of the Kerry Blue Terrier, shall we?

There are two central legends around the Kerry Blue Terrier which both center on shipwrecks. In the first legend, a Spanish Armada is involved, and in the second, it's a Russian shipwreck. Both shipwrecks happened on the coast of Ireland in county Kerry, and the sole survivor in both alleged shipwrecks was a blue dog, who then swam up to dry land, and proceeded to become the ancestor of what we know today as the Kerry Blue Terrier,[8] thanks to romantic entanglements with the local Wheaten Terriers. But of course, these are legends, and the tales may or may not be true. Modern genetics reveal that the Wheaten Terrier is a definite ancestor of the Kerry Blue, but other dogs are also involved in the ancestry chart.

The Kerry Blue Terrier is one of the few Terriers out there who quite enjoy romping around in the water. And, of course, the Kerry Blue Terrier was also renowned for its ability to control pests (the pests were actually referred to as vermin, but I don't know it feels a bit anachronistic to call them that) like rats, as well as hunt birds and rabbits. These dogs develop quite a strong bond with their families and are very sentimental toward them. Trust is a given here—a Kerry Blue's family can always rely on their Kerry Blue Terrier to be affectionate and sensitive to their moods (of course, many other breeds also fit the bill in this regard, but the Kerry Blue Terrier is certainly special in this criteria). An easy lesson to learn from the Kerry Blues is their ability to be sensitive to people's moods—it basically refers to emotional intelligence, which is something good or effective leaders possess. Having the ability to be aware and cognizant of others' moods and emotions is something that will benefit one as a leader (or follower) immensely. That ability to recognize others' emotions and moods and act on them can help the other person trust you and set you up for a good high-quality working relationship.

Another Terrier type I must bring up here is one that does not necessarily have the greatest press out there. I refer to the Staffordshire Bull Terrier,[9,10] often called the Pit Bull Terrier, by the popular press, especially when there is a tragic attack situation involving dogs. No matter what the dog is, the press calls it a Staffordshire Bull Terrier, even when the dog in question has not even any remote connections with Staffordshire Bull Terriers. That is a big pity because this leads to a situation where a few bad apples have destroyed the good name and repute of so many good apples, or dogs as the case is here. There is no denying that there are criminal types of humans out there who shouldn't be allowed to have even a stuffed toy dog let alone a big powerful breed like a Cane Corso or a Staffordshire Bull Terrier or a Rottweiler, etc. That kind of owner typically has dogs that are poorly trained and have poor temperaments, and due to the dual effects of poor ownership and poor temperament, those dogs get involved in tragic incidents, which then have the effects of stereotyping the breeds involved in the attack. The Staffy is unlucky to be the most stereotyped dog[11-13] in that list because of its past as a fighting dog in the bull pits of yore! However, families (consisting of good owners, not the criminal poorly equipped kind) find that their Staffordshire Bull Terriers are practically akin to nannies. Indeed, many decades ago, these dogs practically acted as nanny dogs! The Staffordshire Terrier is even immortalized in literature in the South African book *Jock of the Bushveld*. The book is today considered dated due to the colonial era problematic language used in it, but if you read it as a book about Staffordshire Terriers, you do learn quite a bit about the breed.

This is a dog breed that owners have to be really focused on providing good-quality obedience training, as the dog is fearless. And, fearless is not a quality that goes well with bad or poor-quality training. But if you take care of the training element, these are some of the best dogs one can have in one's family. Well, I suppose, there will always be people on the outside, who may mistrust you and your dog and stereotype against or try to discriminate against you and your Staffy, but that is out of your control—the only way to counter that level of mistrust is to ensure that your Staffordshire Terrier is a model good canine citizen. Over time, people will start to trust your Staffy as much as you trust your Staffy. It is a pity that many Staffy owners find they start in a position of low trust, but that is the tragedy of stereotyping against

82 LEARNING LEADERSHIP FROM DOGS

people or dogs. Stereotypes erode trust, and those being stereotyped have to work extra hard at managing trust.

Another dog breed (a newer one this time, that was only admitted to the AKC in 2004) that one can associate with trust right off the bat is the Black Russian Terrier.[14] This breed was developed by the Soviet government in the USSR back in the 1930s. The overarching purpose was to create a superdog for the Russian army—almost like a dog equivalent situation of creating Captain America or The Winter Soldier. The origins of this breed are interesting— remember, when I had discussed Borzois in Chapter 6, I had mentioned that the breed was in critical danger due to the indiscriminate slaughter executed by the Soviets. They soon realized that their initial zeal had led to a near annihilation of Russian dogs, and with the World War, it was impractical to be thinking of importing dogs from other countries. The initial origin of this breed began with Giant Schnauzers, Airedale Terriers (the King of Terriers, and neatly enough descended from Otterhounds), and Newfoundlands. After the rough beginnings, and after the World War had ended, the scientists were eventually able to get better quality imported dogs, to help refine the breed.

The dog itself was basically used as an all-purpose dog, who could not only patrol the border but also be used as a guard dog in Soviet prisons. Eventually, the dog was introduced to the Russian public and stepped into its role as a guard dog and companion for Russian homes.

This is another breed that is a wonderful trustworthy animal for its family— the dog itself retains a protective instinct, and many of these dogs are used as protective companion dogs. It's also called the Tchiorny Terrier in Russia, but in most other countries, it is simply referred to as the BRT or Black Russian Terrier. Curiously though, the breed only has about 15% Terrier origin, but still, the distinctive Terrier look helps make the name look really apt. This again is a dog whose family can reliably trust the dog to keep a lookout for the well-being of the family. This one time, I met a Black Russian Terrier during a walk in the woods, and he was a fine specimen. A majestic-looking powerful breed, and the owners assured me that he was very protective and incredibly trustworthy.

Jumping gears, a trifle bit, let me now discuss the Giant Schnauzer,[15] which is one of the dog breeds used in the creation of the Black Russian Terrier. This dog looks somewhat similar to the Black Russian Terrier, but yet, if you place them side by side, you can see the subtle differences between the two breeds. In terms of occupations though, both the Giant Schnauzer and the Black Russian Terrier tend to be used as police dogs and tracking dogs, especially for search and rescue operations. This is another impressively intelligent dog, who can be trained with ease. Another very trustworthy breed, which families and law enforcement personnel rely on without any worries. The Giant Schnauzer is an imposing-looking dog, but as long as one gives it enough exercise, it is an easy dog breed to keep and maintain. Of course, when one talks about the Giant Schnauzer, it is only fair to mention the other kinds of Schnauzers—the Mini Schnauzer and the Standard Schnauzer. Both those dogs look similar to the Giant Schnauzer, but of course, are significantly smaller. The Standard Schnauzer unlike the Giant Schnauzer was primarily used as a farm ratter (i.e., used to hunt rats on farms), but of course, is now pretty much employed as a lovable family pet. The Standard Schnauzer is equally trustworthy but it looks like the Miniature Schnauzer is the one that most people recognize. It is one of the most popular dog breeds out there, and indeed, among the Schnauzers it is the undisputed winner in terms of popularity. It usually shows up in the top twenty most popular breeds in the annual AKC lists.

Switching categories, a little, I want to discuss Leonbergers[16] next. These are friendly giants and hail from the town of Leonberg in Germany. They are gentle to the core with their families and want nothing better than to spend time with their owners and families. They are especially gentle with children and similar to the Newfoundland, they are superbly trustworthy around humans at least. Unlike Newfoundlands, they aren't always the best around other dogs. But they can certainly be trusted around other humans, and of course, should their humans need rescuing, you can bet that the Leonberger will spring to the task with its bushy tail. And as I said, these are giant dogs (the big males can weigh up to 170 pounds), which makes them imposing looking, but the amount of trust you can give the Leonberger is proportional to its body size and weight—needless to say, that trust is rather large.

Now that I've discussed several dogs that I think exemplify the quality of trust, as in, them providing plenty of reason to be trusted, I believe a section spelling out how we can improve our own trustworthiness, and increase our overall potential to be trusted by others, is in order.

How Do We Get Others to Trust Us?

Getting others to trust leaders is usually a work in progress—this is especially true for new leaders or for leaders who are working with new followers. This is obvious because, in new work relationships, it takes time to trust the other person. Most people would find it imprudent to trust someone right off the bat. There's always a waiting period prior to being able to trust another person, be it as a leader or as a follower. Let's discuss how we can get others to trust us first.

For starters, the best way to get others to trust us is for us to be consistent and approachable. The consistent aspect is quite straightforward—essentially, people tend to trust people who are consistent and reliable, in all matters, but right now, we're talking specifically about temperament. It's very hard almost impossible to trust a person who is fundamentally unreliable. Let's imagine

84   LEARNING LEADERSHIP FROM DOGS

a person who's pleasant at one instance, and then dramatically changes into an unpleasant individual, and then a few moments later, assumes an air of pleasantness again. That is not a person anyone could trust—imagine having a leader who is like that, that is, mercurial in disposition, and completely unreliable. It would be really difficult to ever get to trust that sort of person. Therefore, I would suggest that individuals desirous of improving their trustworthiness perception work on improving their reliabilities of disposition. That does not mean of course, that one keeps a permanent smile or frown on one's face perennially, just to appear reliable. But it does mean that one tries to be equanimous in all situations, and interactions.

The various dogs I've described in the previous parts of this chapter (and other dogs in other chapters as well, I must add), all possess that equanimity factor in spadesful. That equanimity of temperament is something that can really ramp up one's likeability factor as well as positively affect people's perceptions of a person. Think about it—we tend to trust people who are stable and approachable. If we cannot even approach a person, say that person is an irascible grumpy individual, who would want to approach that person, right? Another attribute which can really help amplify our trustworthiness is the quality of authenticity. If we act in accordance with what we speak, that is, to say, display a good fit between our attitudes and behaviors, then that will help others trust us.

In other words, what we say matters, and we should adhere to what we say or tell others. If we promise something to others, we must do our very best to ensure that we keep our promise. That may not always be possible, of course, but in that case, we must at least strive to communicate clearly about why failure to keep the promise occurred. Sometimes people can get embarrassed at their failure to keep a promise, and their gut reaction is to avoid the person who they failed to deliver on their promise with. That avoidance inevitably leads to a worse relationship because now not only does the person know that there was a broken promise but also it is worse now because of the silence and ghosting of a sort that ensues. I would suggest that we rely on clear communication even in times when promises are broken, or some deliverables are just not delivered. Clear communication with more explanation of why the promise was broken can go a long way in mending any breach of trust.

Another way to get people to trust you is to be visible and present. It is harder to trust someone who is never available to meet with or even to see around. Imagine you have a boss who rarely shows up to work and is never available to meet with you or to confer with you—that's not going to inspire you much if at all. On the contrary, it's probably going to lead you to distrust your boss. How do you trust someone who's never available or visible? While you don't want someone breathing down your neck, you do want the mental assurance that if you need your boss, you'll be able to get in touch with him or her.

That visibility and presence combined with equanimity of temperament can help you be perceived as more trustworthy by others.

Yet another way to increase others' trust on you involves a slightly convoluted reciprocity principle. Basically, to get people to trust you, you have to put yourself in a place of vulnerability. By that I mean, you have to trust people and show them that you trust them, in order to get them to reciprocate trust back to you. I know it sounds a tad bit circular, but it's really not. The principle of reciprocity is one where we feel obliged to reciprocate someone's good gesture—in some instances, we mirror or mimic their body language, and that's done implicitly, with no real thought to it. We've also heard about and perhaps even experienced the contagious yawning syndrome, where one person's yawn sets off other people to yawn too. All that falls into the realms of reciprocity, and applying that principle to trust is quite logical. If you show that you trust another person, then unless that person is a hardened sociopath or a highly Machiavellian individual, that person will return the trust back. In short, we have to trust others to get them to trust us—this is especially true in burgeoning relationships, where there isn't enough history to allow for a mutually trusting relationship.

Why Though?

This question possibly does arise in many of your minds—okay, sure, we have this list of dogs that exemplify trust, and we also have a pretty good idea about how to become more trustworthy ourselves. But why exactly is it important to be trustworthy leaders, even without being trustworthy, leaders could use their positional power to demand compliance from their followers. Sure, compliance could be obtained through coercion, but whatever compliance is obtained is bound to be rather temporary, because nobody (well okay, almost nobody) likes being coerced into doing things, at least not on a permanent basis.

We tend to like people we trust (and vice versa), and we also tend to be more committed to helping or aiding people we trust. So, let's say as a leader you have a vision in mind—sure, you could coerce or force someone to comply into behaving a certain way for you to reach that vision. But think about how things could be drastically improved if the person who's aiding you does so wholeheartedly and with commitment.[17] The quality of work that will result in the presence of commitment will be infinitely better than the quality of work that will result due to coercion. And not only that, if leaders trust their followers, the amount of stress that the leader takes on will be drastically reduced too. Being a leader is often fraught with a whole host of anxieties, and trust is the balm to soothe away many-an-anxiety. And it goes the other way too—being a follower isn't necessarily always a bed of roses. There are plenty of anxieties that followers must face too, and if they find that they are able to trust their leaders, their own anxieties could be lessened or perhaps even eliminated.

Trustworthiness in a leader has been found to influence many positive outcomes from an organizational or personal perspective. For instance, trustworthiness in a leader often results in a reduction in turnover and an uptick in commitment.[18-20] It also results in an increase in cooperation among coworkers, higher job satisfaction, and even better performance. Similarly, trustworthiness in followers can help leaders focus on the larger vision in mind, and not get distracted by minor. So, to state it all succinctly, trust is a quality that we must learn to not only use on others but also have others attribute it to us.

Summary

In this chapter, I discuss the concept of trust and outline why it is important for individuals to inspire others to trust in them, and also be able to trust others the way they would like them to trust them. I have discussed dog breeds like the Staffordshire Terrier, Black Russian Terrier, and Giant Schnauzer among others in the context of trust. I have also briefly discussed ways by which we can get others to start trusting us. In Chapter 9, I will be discussing the topic of intelligence, and discuss and describe several dog breeds that exemplify intelligence.

Kerry Blue Terrier   Staffordshire Bull Terrier

Black Russian Terrier   Standard Schnauzer

Giant Schnauzer

Miniature Schnauzer

Leonberger

Airedale Terrier

References

1 Soderberg, A. T., & Romney, A. C. (2022). Building trust: How leaders can engender feelings of trust among followers. *Business Horizons*, 65(2), 173–182.
2 Breevaart, K., & Zacher, H. (2019). Main and interactive effects of weekly transformational and laissez-faire leadership on followers' trust in the leader and leader effectiveness. *Journal of Occupational and Organizational Psychology*, 92(2), 384–409.
3 Kohles, J. C., Bligh, M. C., & Carsten, M. K. (2012). A follower-centric approach to the vision integration process. *The Leadership Quarterly*, 23(3), 476–487.
4 Burke, C. S., Sims, D. E., Lazzara, E. H., & Salas, E. (2007). Trust in leadership: A multi-level review and integration. *The Leadership Quarterly*, 18(6), 606–632.
5 Ryan, S., & Cross, C. (2024). Micromanagement and its impact on millennial followership styles. *Leadership & Organization Development Journal*, 45(1), 140–152.
6 Irani-Williams, F., Tribble, L., Rutner, P. S., Campbell, C., McKnight, D. H., & Hardgrave, B. C. (2021). Just let me do my job! Exploring the impact of micromanagement on IT professionals. *ACM SIGMIS Database: The DATABASE for Advances in Information Systems*, 52(3), 77–95.
7 https://www.thekennelclub.org.uk/search/breeds-a-to-z/breeds/terrier/kerry-blue-terrier.
8 https://www.akc.org/expert-advice/dog-breeds/kerry-blue-terrier-history/.
9 https://www.akc.org/dog-breeds/staffordshire-bull-terrier/.

88 LEARNING LEADERSHIP FROM DOGS

10 https://www.thekennelclub.org.uk/search/breeds-a-to-z/breeds/terrier/staffordshire-bull-terrier/.

11 Patronek, G., Twining, H., & Arluke, A. (2000). Managing the stigma of outlaw breeds: A case study of pit bull owners. *Society & Animals*, 8(1), 25–52.

12 Duberstein, A., King, B., & Johnson, A. R. (2023). Pit bulls and prejudice. *The Humanistic Psychologist*, 51(2), 183–188.

13 Steinert, K., Kuhne, F., Kramer, M., & Hackbarth, H. (2019). People's perception of brachycephalic breeds and breed-related welfare problems in Germany. *Journal of Veterinary Behavior*, 33, 96–102.

14 https://www.akc.org/dog-breeds/black-russian-terrier/.

15 https://www.akc.org/dog-breeds/giant-schnauzer/.

16 https://www.akc.org/dog-breeds/leonberger/.

17 Yang, J., & Mossholder, K. W. (2010). Examining the effects of trust in leaders: A bases-and-foci approach. *The Leadership Quarterly*, 21(1), 50–63.

18 Podsakoff, P. M., MacKenzie, S. B., Moorman, R. H., & Fetter, R. (1990). Transformational leader behaviors and their effects on followers' trust in leader, satisfaction, and organizational citizenship behaviors. *The Leadership Quarterly*, 1(2), 107–142.

19 Costigan, R. D., Insinga, R., Berman, J. J., Kranas, G., & Kureshov, V. A. (2013). The significance of direct-leader and co-worker trust on turnover intentions: A cross-cultural study. *Journal of Trust Research*, 3(2), 98–124.

20 Costigan, R. D., Insinga, R. C., Berman, J. J., Kranas, G., & Kureshov, V. A. (2011). Revisiting the relationship of supervisor trust and CEO trust to turnover intentions: A three-country comparative study. *Journal of World Business*, 46(1), 74–83.

Chapter 9

INU INTELLIGENCE

In the very beginning, when I first envisaged this book, I hadn't initially thought about having a separate chapter on intelligence. But as time went ticking along and the book started to come together, I figured it would be clinically insane not to have a chapter on intelligence. So, here we are—a chapter on intelligence, and this of course is another quality that is vital for successful leadership. Sometimes you can have intelligent leaders do something unintelligent, but the simple fact remains that it is far unlikelier for an unintelligent leader to do something intelligent. Just by dint of pure luck, an unintelligent leader may do something intelligent, but it is rather unlikely in most situations. However, by the same yardstick, intelligence isn't always universal—there are times when one form of intelligence works better than another form of intelligence, and leaders often have to choose which kind of intelligence they need to rely on given a situation.

There is a plethora of types of intelligence, and a majority of them can be categorized into either cognitive intelligence or emotional intelligence types.[1-3] I will be focusing the discussion and explanation in this chapter around these two main categories of intelligence. In some ways, the conversation around intelligence parallels the conversation around the nature versus nurture element of leadership. There are some who believe that intelligence is something people are born with, while others believe that intelligence is something people can and do learn.[4-6] I will argue that the truth (like most things in life) is somewhere in the middle. There are elements of intelligence that we are naturally gifted at, and there are elements of intelligence that we have to work at in order to improve. This chapter posed a wee bit of a struggle for me to be able to decide which dogs to write about here, as there are far too many breeds which I could talk about. Some of the intelligent breeds have already been discussed in preceding chapters (e.g., German Shepherds, Poodles, etc.), and it is my aim to discuss wholly unique breeds in every chapter. Else, we'd be running the risk of having the entire book focus on Otterhounds and Dachshunds, which would be jolly for those breed lovers, but not so jolly for other breed fanciers.

90   LEARNING LEADERSHIP FROM DOGS

As is the norm in this book, I will feature and discuss several dog breeds, who I believe exemplify intelligence of various sorts, and I will also discuss ways by which we ourselves can improve our own intelligence levels. All dogs are incredibly intelligent, although, their intelligence does take on different flavors and flairs, very much like humans. And to be effective leaders, we have to know when to employ various kinds of intelligence. For instance, a person being brilliant in mathematics does not mean that the person is equally gifted in dramatics. To sign up that person for a dramatics competition on dint of his or her intelligence in math is not a very intelligent decision. So, let me first start off with a little bit of discussion on the different kinds of intelligence out there, while first focusing on cognitive intelligence.

The In(u)'s of Cognitive Intelligence

Let us embark on a journey first to discuss what exactly comprises intelligence. The word itself has a plethora of definitions, but all of the definitions have an element of being able to process information (whatever the type of information is determines the intelligence type). For instance, if one has a high level of understanding and knowledge about differential calculus, that indicates the person has a high level of cognitive intelligence. That particular kind of intelligence is one of the earliest studied forms of intelligence. Remember the once-ubiquitous IQ (intelligence quotient) tests? That is directly a measure of cognitive intelligence, and it was considered to be the most important form of intelligence. IQ tests were first developed around 1905 (while the research around them started off in the mid-1890s). Alfred Binet is usually credited as being the first inventor of the modern IQ test—the original test was created in order to help the French government assess which children would require extra help at school to be successful. This original test was then modified and standardized with an American sample of respondents and called the Stanford–Binet test, which also helped popularize the IQ score.[7-9] The original test has since been revised and made more complex in order to be justifiable psychometrically speaking.

IQ tests were often used to make hiring and promotion decisions,[10] but more importantly, prior to that function, they were used to make immigration decisions.[11] Imagine immigrating to a new country, not being fluent in the language or knowing its customs, and getting entire groups prohibited from immigrating there due to having "inferior" IQ scores. That actually led to many groups being discriminated against by the US Congress from an immigration perspective. This sounds rather galling because today we know that IQ tests are not the end-all determinants of intelligence. Indeed, a lot of IQ tests are biased against some groups of people. Take for instance, the group of immigrants who were discriminated against when they tried to immigrate to the United States in the early twentieth century—only those individuals who were fluent in English did well on the IQ tests. Imagine taking an IQ test in a language which is unfamiliar to you—you probably wouldn't do very well in it either. Let's say you have to take an IQ test which is administered in the Khalkha Mongolian language, and this is the first time you've even heard of the language. I can guarantee that you will be unlikely to do very well on this test, which could lead the evaluator to suggest your IQ score is low. This is pretty similar to what happened to the early immigrants who did poorly on IQ tests, not only were they adjudicated as being low IQ individuals, but other people from their ethnic backgrounds or national origins were also castigated as being low IQ.

Ultimately, one's success on an IQ test depends on how much knowledge or familiarity one has with the language the test is being administered in. Also, depending on the specifics of the test, there might be certain elements of the test that are problematic for certain groups of people. For instance, someone who has an issue with concentration, would not do very well on a regular IQ test. They may be supremely cognitively intelligent, but their test scores will not indicate that proficiency, simply because they lost focus and stopped concentrating on the test at hand. Individuals with ADHD, for instance, would find it very hard to sit through a lengthy IQ test. I bring up this point here because this is one point that directly correlates to dogs' cognitive intelligence—while all dogs are to a certain extent intelligent, there are some that excel at certain tasks while others don't. Then whoever is interpreting or evaluating the results calls the dogs that don't comply unintelligent. They don't take the time to properly evaluate whether their assessment was correctly assessed or not. Imagine trying to get a French Bulldog to swim the length of a deep swimming pool, and then giving it failing marks for poor swimming, despite realizing that the dog really isn't built to be a swimmer.

Now, let's talk about some dogs that rate really high on cognitive intelligence. These are smart dogs that can accomplish a lot, and get accolades for being highly trainable dogs.

Let's start off with a dog from down under, namely the Australian Shepherd.[12,13] Actually, scratch that, turns out the Australian Shepherd is a dog breed developed in the US, primarily as a ranch dog. Its ancestors' human families originated in Australia, but then they immigrated to the US, and the breed was further developed. This breed is one of the most intelligent and gifted dogs out there. Highly trainable and incredibly work-oriented.

Aussie Shepherds are excellent herding dogs and driven with a zeal to please. There is a downside of having this much intelligence though—if an Australian Shepherd isn't given enough mental exercise, they can become restless and sadly engage in destructive behaviors. In many ways, this parallels what happens when you have humans with high IQ levels, who are not given any opportunity to use that smartness—they turn to destructive pastimes. A lot of delinquency among the youth across nations can be traced to this lack of opportunity. But anyway, when it comes to high-IQ dogs, Australian Shepherds are definitely in the upper echelon of that group.

Passing on from Australia [...] err [...] America, let's go to the rugged Shetland Islands in Scotland. The breed that I'll talk about next is the Shetland Sheepdog,[14,15] which looks for all purposes like a miniature Rough Collie (discussed back in Chapter 4). The dog was initially named the Shetland Collie, but the larger Collie breeders forced a name change to the Sheepdog, as they didn't want their breed name diluted.[16] But the dogs are not exactly the same either—there are some similarities and some dissimilarities between the cousins.

However, due to the complete lack of written records, it is very difficult to say when exactly Collies were brought into the Shetland Islands, and miniaturized so to speak. But the link between Shelties and their larger cousins is definitely unmistakable. The Shetland Sheepdog is another incredibly intelligent dog breed—it is easily trained and needs plenty of intellectual stimulation like the Aussie does. If these dogs get bored, they start to engage in destructive behaviors just like the Aussies. But if you can get to train them with patience and a sense of fun, Shelties can practically do anything. There's a Sheltie duo I knew once, and they were two of the smartest dogs I ever met. They could do tricks like no other dog could, and their owner told me that he had the easiest time training those Shelties.

Another dog I must discuss here in the context of cognitive intelligence is the Indian Spitz.[17] This is not a dog breed recognized by the AKC, but having grown up in India in the 1990s, this was an immensely popular and recognizable breed. In those days, the most common trio of dog breeds were the Indian Spitz (often incorrectly called the Pomeranian), German Shepherd, and Dobermann Pinscher. This was due to strict and restrictive rules in importing foreign dogs into India—today, the situation is much different. Breeds wholly unsuited for the Indian climate or condition are now found easily across the country. Can you imagine how horrible life must be for a Saint Bernard in a hot muggy climate? Of course, you could keep one in a 24/7 airconditioned house, but I'm not sure the dog would enjoy it as much. Rather like a canary in a gilded cage, after all!

But anyway, returning back to the Indian Spitz now. I do feel a bit compelled to bring this dog into the narrative here, due to how ubiquitous the breed was during my days of youth. There was an Indian Spitz my maternal grandparents and uncles had when I was a breezy boy—the dog's name was

INU INTELLIGENCE   93

Sweety, although I used to call her Snowy (being a fan of Tintin). She was a nice dog and very intelligent. I wish I had more memories of her though—I only knew her for a few months. Anyway, the breed itself is descended from the German Spitz, although it is a smaller version of the German Spitz, and the Indian Spitz tends to be mostly white in color. This is another highly intelligent breed and responds really well to fun training and can be trained to perform a variety of tricks and tasks. I remember seeing contingents of Indian Spitzes in Indian circuses performing a variety of tricks and would marvel at seeing how well they performed.

They were the equivalent of Poodles in European or American circuses, but as I said, due to stringent import conditions, Indian circuses had to rely on the Indian Spitzes instead. It was a bit annoying though when I'd see an Indian Spitz that was completely untrained and left to roam around loose—it was such a waste of the potential that those intelligent dogs had. Cognitive intelligence is a great asset, but only if one actually harnesses it. Today, the Indian Spitz is a noticeably rarer breed to see across India, but those that remain still possess a great deal of cognitive intelligence—hopefully, the owners that have them today make the effort to harness their incredible intelligence.

Going along with the Spitz motif, let us pass along now to a Dutch breed, namely the Keeshond.[18] This is another Spitz variety but from Holland and is often given the nickname "The Smiling Dutchman" due to its country of origin and its naturally smiling visage. The Keeshond used to be a river dog, as in, used to be kept by the boatmen who operated barges on the rivers in Holland. This is yet another hugely intelligent dog, which is always eager to learn new things too. That quality is something I wish more people had in ample quantities—I refer to the hunger to learn more. It's not simply enough to possess cognitive intelligence, you have to want to use it and grow it too. The Keeshond has ample quantities of that aptitude for learning, which goes very well with its already high intelligence. This is also a breed that is of a very amiable sort and gets along well with people and other pets.

This other breed I am pretty much including this at the request of my older son, Advi, who quite insisted that I include this breed into the book somewhere or the other. Well, no better place than here to introduce the Castro Laboreiro Dog[19] or the Portuguese Cattle Dog. This is a pretty rare dog to find outside of its native Portugal and is renowned for being an intelligent and loyal dog, which originally was a livestock guardian but has of late become a companion and protection dog in Portugal. It is quite renowned in its native Portugal but somehow hasn't made the transatlantic leap into global popularity yet. It looks like we might need to make a trip to Portugal in the near future to see one of these dogs up close.

94   LEARNING LEADERSHIP FROM DOGS

Before cruising along to emotional intelligence and some of its subtypes, I do want to also discuss a few breeds who are not necessarily thought of as cognitively gifted dogs. Let me start off with the Afghan Hound.[20] For years, I've been reading about how stupid Afghan Hounds are, and how poorly they fare on canine intelligence tests. On many tests, the Afghan Hound placed squarely at last, which led people to call the Afghan Hound the dunce in the canine kingdom. Let me take this opportunity to denounce that particular interpretation—the Afghan Hound is not a stupid or idiotic or unintelligent breed. It is quite cognitively intelligent, what it lacks is a desire to perform tricks or follow instructions it sees no value for. This is almost like how school systems sometimes grade neurodivergent children harshly for not doing well on their standardized tests—it's not like the children aren't cognitively gifted, it's just that the tests don't do a good job of testing what they're supposedly testing. The Afghan Hound's reputation has been sullied due to that dunce image, which is quite undeserving.

In reality, the Afghan Hound is a beautiful elegant, and powerful hound dog. Take a look at its luxurious silky coat, which is not just for strutting around in a dog show—the reason for that coat lies in the origins of the breed. The dog needed a coat like that for the harsh and cold winters of Afghanistan. This breed is perhaps a lot more special than other breeds in that it requires a special sort of fit between owner and dog. Not everyone can keep and be happy with an Afghan Hound, but for those, who match the dignified yet dotted with a streak of silliness in its temperament. This breed has always been known to have independence in thinking, and with plenty of stubbornness to boot. It also tends to be really loyal to its owners and is very difficult to rehome, due to that loyalty. But it is certainly not cognitively unintelligent, as the various canine intelligence tests done in the past attested. Indeed, the Afghan Hound excels in lure coursing, which was never even an option on that canine IQ test on which the Afghan Hounds emerged as bottom of the pack.

Similar to the Afghan Hound, there is a dog breed originating from Japan, called the Shiba Inu.[21] Even if you're not really up with your ken of dog breeds, you'll recognize the Shiba Inu, thanks to the cryptocurrency Dogecoin, which features a smiley Shiba Inu as the mascot of Dogecoin. While the cryptocurrency has been pretty inconsistent, the Shiba Inu itself has been a very popular Japanese dog. It is the most popular Japanese-origin breed of dog and has been gaining popularity in the US and several parts of Europe. The name of the dog basically refers to its red color or the color of brushwood in the mountains, since Shiba literally translates to Brushwood. This is another cognitively intelligent dog, and anyone who really dreads the housebreaking aspect of dogs should certainly consider a Shiba Inu (this is one of the easiest dog breeds to housebreak). However, this is also a dog who

INU INTELLIGENCE 95

is super independent thinking and will not hesitate to go wandering if he/ she wants to. There is only so much obedience training that Shiba Inus will respond to, and their independent streak will probably demote them on a standard canine intelligence test.

Another dog that comes to mind when discussing cognitive intelligence is the Briard,[22] which hails from France. This is a large French dog, who is a master of herding and guarding sheep. They have a beautiful long thick coat, and a luxurious beard to go with it, and are very affectionate and protective of children in the family (they consider children to be part of their flock). Now the Briard too will also probably not top the list in terms of IQ on the canine IQ test, but that's a function of what they were bred to do. As herders and guardian dogs, Briards often have to make executive decisions on the fly, so a certain independence of thinking is naturally found in Briards. That does make it a tad bit difficult to train, but as long as you can come up with a fun-training regimen, the Briard will excel at training, and indeed, can be trained to accomplish a variety of tasks including canine sports or search-and-rescue.

I've used these dogs as examples to talk about cognitive intelligence, and also discuss how cognitive intelligence tests aren't exactly all that accurate. This next section will involve discussing emotional intelligence, and a few of its subtypes, after which, I will discuss certain dog breeds that I think are very reflective of emotional intelligence.

The In(u)'s of Emotional Intelligence

The preceding section was all about cognitive intelligence—this one is going to be about emotional intelligence. Unlike its cognitive counterpart, emotional intelligence deals not only with the ability to manage your own emotions but also be able to understand and comprehend others' emotions.[23] In today's era, and indeed since the early 2000s, emotional intelligence has become much more important than the previously vaunted cognitive intelligence. Essentially, emotional intelligence has to do with being able to manage people through their many moods and emotions. If you think of the comedy show The Big Bang Show, you begin to see the differences between cognitive and emotional intelligence. In the show, all the main characters are high on cognitive intelligence, but pretty low on emotional intelligence, which rather stymies their overall life experiences. It is the same case for leaders who may be high on cognitive intelligence, but glaringly low on emotional intelligence. Just cognitive intelligence alone is rarely enough, they do need a modicum of emotional intelligence to be able to be truly effective. After all, leadership is all about leading and influencing others—one cannot do that well if one does not understand or read people's moods and emotions.

96   LEARNING LEADERSHIP FROM DOGS

Another related intelligence type is social intelligence[24]—this form of intelligence deals with the ability to handle people in social situations. One learns from one's past failures and successes in social situations and uses that to develop one's own sense of social intelligence. Individuals with good social intelligence tend to be better in social situations when dealing with people, and as one can tell, this is a definite bonus quality that leaders ought to possess.

Leaders are usually busy interacting with other people, be the other leaders or followers or nonorganizational actors. It is important for the leader to be able to handle social situations with aplomb. And let us be frank here—social situations have so much complexity that it can be difficult to be truly exceptional in every possible social situation. But it is important to try to be so in every social situation.

The main way by which leaders or even nonleaders can improve their emotional and social intelligence is to pay attention to what and how others respond to them. It is important to pay heed to others' emotions and truly listen to what they are really communicating. That is the essence of emotional intelligence and of its subtype, social intelligence. There is another form of intelligence called cultural intelligence,[25] which measures one's aptitude to relate with others and work effectively in culturally diverse contexts. As you can see, all of these forms of intelligence are linked with emotional intelligence. In the end, it all boils down to how well a person can read another person, and how well one knows oneself, and one's own response to others. Now dogs actually fit very well into all of these various forms of emotional intelligence—dogs are so in tune with human emotions. We've all seen our dogs commiserate with us when we're sad or gloomy, and we've seen them join in on the fun when we're exuberant, etc. Dogs can really read humans a lot better than humans can read themselves. I will now discuss a few more dog breeds, especially those that I feel excel in the emotional intelligence dimension.

Let's begin with Belgium this time around—in particular, a really intelligent dog breed, the Schipperke.[26] The name literally means "Little Captain," and refers to the breed's history being a traditional barge dog. Like some of the other dogs I mentioned in the cognitive category, the Schipperke is equally independent minded and loves going off roaming if given half a chance. This is another Spitz dog and is a unique foxy-looking dog, which needs a lot of intellectual and physical stimulation. However, where this dog really shines is in knowing how to read emotions. The Schipperke has a high level of emotional intelligence because it really harnesses its natural alertness and leverages that into appropriate behavioral responses. Very much reflective of emotional intelligence, that.

Moving along to France, let us espy the beautiful Papillon,[27] which is named for its erect and fringed ears, which resemble butterfly wings. This

INU INTELLIGENCE   97

was a very popular breed in the royal courts of Europe and was later imported
to France in the 1700s, where it became a raging success once again. This
is another dog that is not only cognitively gifted, but also gifted emotional
intelligence wise. The Papillon is a master at assessing its owner's emotions,
and if it determines that some amount of commiseration is required, it happily
springs to the task. For being such a small dog, the Papillon has a large heart
(figuratively speaking), and we can all learn loads from the Papillon on how
to read human emotions accurately. A rather grisly historical fact also unveils
the depth of loyalty that the Papillon bestows on its owner.

Remember the hapless Queen Mary Antoinette, who is the French
Revolution fame—she had a pet Papillon (named Thisbe) who faithfully
awaited her outside her prison.[28] Sadly, for Thisbe, the Queen did not survive
the French Revolution but that incident does make me feel a bit sad, for both
Thisbe and the Queen.

Another dog breed that exemplifies emotional intelligence is the super
intelligent and good-natured Bichon Frise.[29] This dog showcases both
cognitive and emotional intelligence and is a pleasure to train as well. The
Bichon also loves to perform tricks for its family and admire passersby.
This breed too was a huge hit with the Royals, but the French Revolution
brought an abrupt and grisly end to most of the dog's fanciers. As a result, the
Bichons had to fend for themselves in the street. Eventually, street performers
discovered that the Bichons were tremendous performers, and they soon
got reputed as circus-performing dogs. Imagine going from a royal palace
to an altogether different environment, and still thriving despite the sudden
change in circumstances? That demonstrates how emotionally and socially
intelligent Bichon Frises is to be able to get along great with both royalty as
well as common folks.

The final dog that I'll talk about in this chapter is the Wire Fox Terrier.[30]
I love this breed and have been a fan and admirer of this dog breed since early
childhood. While growing up, I was an avid reader and fan of the Tintin
series, and still am to be honest. It is a Belgian comic series featuring an
intrepid reporter and investigator, with his intelligent companion dog, Snowy.
The dog in question, that is, Snowy happens to be a wholly white Wire Fox
Terrier. In reality though, you rarely ever see an all-white Wire Fox Terrier.
Usually, they happen to be Red and White. This is another lovely breed and
super fun to have in one's home. Another superbly intelligent dog, and one
that can easily understand and read its owner's emotions. Curiously though,
this dog's country of origin is England, even though, Tintin himself was
written to be of Belgian origin. The Wire Fox Terrier is an eternally upbeat
character, who is also very skilled at understanding what their owners and
family members are feeling. This dog is adept at comedy and often conjures

98 LEARNING LEADERSHIP FROM DOGS

up funny tricks to make gloom or boredom disappear. Again, the level of intelligence a Wire Fox Terrier possesses is quite sublimely high, and indeed, it has high levels of both cognitive and emotional intelligence.

Putting It All Together

Now that I've covered the two main types of intelligence, it does seem worthwhile to put it all together and lay out how exactly it pertains to leaders. I would argue that both cognitive and emotional intelligence are necessary qualities in effective leaders—without the former form of intelligence, leaders cannot begin to understand the complexity of various contexts. Consider hiring someone with zero expertise or knowledge to be the leader of a nuclear powerplant. While it is true that the individual may turn out to be lucky and avoid any catastrophes, the truth is that having cognitive intelligence can help leaders navigate crises. If a crisis were to develop under the watch of someone who is not cognitively equipped for the job at hand, then the crisis could probably go longer. We see this in governments across the world—oftentimes, public policy ends up getting dictated by someone with zero functional domain knowledge. How can someone who is an anti-vaxxer end up dictating public policies on vaccines? Well, it sounds unfathomable but there are plenty of individuals like that around occupying prime spots and being pretty useless for the job concerned. It's not that they lack cognitive intelligence (although for the science-denying bunch, that may be a true statement), it's just that they lack domain knowledge or domain-specific cognitive intelligence.

You can get away from needing domain-specific knowledge a bit when it comes to emotional, social, or cultural intelligence. After all, these forms of intelligence are much more aligned with people skills than with technical or domain skills. And in the end, most people are similar—while they may have cultural differences, in the end, all people, regardless of where they're from want to be liked and respected, treated fairly, and reassured if they're feeling fearful or stressed. If leaders can lead people by keeping that in mind, then they've already gotten a huge head start on displaying their high emotional intelligence levels. This is something you can really observe and learn from dogs—their skills at reading the emotions of humans are unparalleled.

From a cognitive intelligence perspective, there's only so much a person can do to increase their levels. After all, you cannot become a math genius by practicing math equations, but you can still improve your knowledge of math, even if you never become a genius. Ditto with other domains—you may not be naturally gifted at a certain domain, but if you happen to work in that domain or field, then at least have the willingness to learn about it.

Some tips to improve cognitive intelligence include playing brain games and strategy games such as chess. It won't increase your domain knowledge, but at least will keep you cognitively sharp. So, just to succinctly state here—there are plenty of dogs who display high levels of both cognitive and emotional intelligence, and they can teach us a lot. The ability to read other people's emotions and also recognize one's own, and act in accordance with that, allows one to make decisions that are optimal and help improve and refine one's leadership effectiveness.

Summary

In this chapter, I discuss the concept of intelligence and outline why it is important for individuals and leaders to have both cognitive intelligence as well as emotional intelligence. I have discussed dog breeds like the Australian Shepherd, Shetland Sheepdog, Afghan Hound, Indian Spitz, Papillon, and the Wire Fox Terrier, among others, in the context of both forms of intelligence. I have also discussed how leaders should ideally aim to improve their own levels of cognitive and emotional intelligence. In the next chapter, I will be discussing the topic of joy or happiness, and discuss and describe several dog breeds that exemplify the quality of joy.

Australian Shepherd   Shetland Sheepdog

Indian Spitz   Keeshond

INU INTELLIGENCE 101

References

1 Brody, N. (2004). What cognitive intelligence is and what emotional intelligence is not. *Psychological Inquiry*, 15(3), 234–238.

2 Côté, S., & Miners, C. T. (2006). Emotional intelligence, cognitive intelligence, and job performance. *Administrative Science Quarterly*, 51(1), 1–28.

3 Ackert, L. F., Deaves, R., Miele, J., & Nguyen, Q. (2020). Are time preference and risk preference associated with cognitive intelligence and emotional intelligence? *Journal of Behavioral Finance*, 21(2), 136–156.

4 Johnson, A. M., Vernon, P. A., McCarthy, J. M., Molson, M., Harris, J. A., & Jang, K. L. (1998). Nature vs nurture: Are leaders born or made? A behavior genetic investigation of leadership style. *Twin Research and Human Genetics*, 1(4), 216–223.

5 Turner, S., & Tsang, Y. (2023). Nature versus nurture: What underpins great leadership? The case for nurture. *Clinical Oncology*, 35(1), 6–9.

6 De Neve, J. E., Mikhaylov, S., Dawes, C. T., Christakis, N. A., & Fowler, J. H. (2013). Born to lead? A twin design and genetic association study of leadership role occupancy. *The Leadership Quarterly*, 24(1), 45–60.

7 Harwood, J. (1983). The IQ in history. *Social Studies of Science*, 13(3), 465–477.

8 Fass, P. S. (1980). The IQ: A cultural and historical framework. *American Journal of Education*, 88(4), 431–458.

9 Siegler, R. S. (1992). The other Alfred Binet. *Developmental Psychology*, 28(2), 179–190.

10 Richardson, K., & Norgate, S. H. (2015). Does IQ really predict job performance? *Applied Developmental Science*, 19(3), 153–169.

11 Snyderman, M., & Herrnstein, R. J. (1983). Intelligence tests and the Immigration Act of 1924. *American Psychologist*, 38(9), 986.

12 https://www.akc.org/dog-breeds/australian-shepherd/.

13 https://www.thekennelclub.org.uk/search/breeds-a-to-z/breeds/pastoral/australian-shepherd/.

14 https://www.thekennelclub.org.uk/search/breeds-a-to-z/breeds/pastoral/shetland-sheepdog/.

15 https://www.akc.org/dog-breeds/shetland-sheepdog/.

16 https://www.akc.org/expert-advice/dog-breeds/shetland-sheepdog-history/.

17 https://vetic.in/blog/breed/the-charismatic-and-popular-indian-spitz/.

18 https://www.akc.org/dog-breeds/keeshond/.

19 https://www.cpc.pt/en/breeds/portuguese-breeds/castro-laboreiro-dog/.

20 https://www.akc.org/dog-breeds/afghan-hound/.

21 https://www.akc.org/dog-breeds/shiba-inu/.

22 https://www.akc.org/dog-breeds/briard/.

23 Northouse, P. G. (2021). *Leadership: Theory and Practice*. Thousand Oaks, California: Sage Publications.

24 Walker, R. E., & Foley, J. M. (1973). Social intelligence: Its history and measurement. *Psychological Reports*, 33(3), 839–864.

25 Earley, P. C., & Mosakowski, E. (2004). Cultural intelligence. *Harvard Business Review*, 82(10), 139–146.

26 https://www.akc.org/dog-breeds/schipperke/.

27 https://www.akc.org/dog-breeds/papillon/.

28 https://www.mariegossip.com/2011/08/pups-of-past-marie-antoinettes-dogs.html.

29 https://www.akc.org/dog-breeds/bichon-frise/.

30 https://www.akc.org/dog-breeds/wire-fox-terrier/.

Chapter 10

PE(E)KING(ESE) AT JOIE DE VIVRE

Joie de vivre is a French expression which basically refers to an attitude of exuberant enjoyment of life. Or in other words, to simply delight in life—to not simply pursue happiness but instead to be happy. This is an attitude that very few people seem to possess—look around you, no really, take a look around you. I can bet it'll be hard to find or spot people who live with an attitude of joie de vivre. The various trials and tribulations of life can certainly beat the joy out of one's life, but it is really so important to strive to retain that joy for life, or else we run the risk of becoming mere hollow versions of ourselves. What's the point of earning money or having material riches, if one doesn't even relish or experience a joyous existence?

Think about the grumpy joyless bosses or leaders or coworkers or any sort of people you may have interacted with in the past (or even have currently)—it isn't much fun to work with individuals like that, is it? Misery begets misery, as the old saying goes. There is some research too that suggests that joyless or unhappy leaders tend to be ineffective leaders—after all, if you have a gloomy joyless Squidward for a boss, you wouldn't necessarily be happy yourself, would you? There is a journal called the *Journal of Happiness Studies* which focuses on topics like happiness, subjective wellbeing, and other related variables. If you peruse the articles through the various issues of that journal, you will begin to see how very important happiness or joy is for a variety of outcomes, be they personal, organizational, or societal outcomes.

Now dogs are quite definitely the best at exemplifying this undying spirit of joie de vivre. Think about your own pet (if you are fortunate enough to have one), and remember how he or she treats you jubilantly when you get back home from work. And then when you prepare to go out for a walk or a hike with your dog; if your dog is like a majority of dogs out there, then he or she will probably bounce about the house or at least politely wait with eager anticipation. Both reactions will demonstrate ample quantities of that beautiful joie de vivre. We don't often grant or express that same joyous attitude to the important others in our lives, be it our personal or our professional lives. I definitely think this joie de vivre attitude is something we

104   LEARNING LEADERSHIP FROM DOGS

ought to learn from dogs, and I firmly believe that it will improve our lives immensely, and make us better persons and leaders. This chapter too posed a bit of a quandary because there are so many dogs that fit the bill to use as exemplars of this attitude, but as is the norm in this book, I'm going to pick the dog breeds that I haven't already picked in previous chapters.

Some Dogs Who Exemplify Joie De Vivre

There are so many dogs out there who exemplify joie de vivre—chances are pretty high that you know a dog like that yourself. I would say all dogs exemplify this attitude, but that would not be completely accurate. There are a few breeds that are a bit more standoffish and gloomier, and there are always exceptions with individual dogs from the joyous breeds as well. But in general, the dogs I'm going to discuss now reflect that joyous attitude in spadesful measures. Let's begin with the toothy Boston Terrier[1]—as the name suggests, this amiable and joyous dog hails from Boston. The Boston Terrier is not only a lively friendly sort but is also an impeccably well-mannered dog. One of the nicknames given to the Boston Terrier is "The American Gentleman," although I suppose female Bostons are nicknamed as "American Ladies." Anyhow, the Boston Terrier walks in a literal bouncy and jaunty way and never fails to bring joy to other people around. As I mentioned in the beginning, misery is contagious, but so too is jubilation. If you have a Boston Terrier, you will be forced to laugh at your dog's antics, even if you're in a bad or upset mood. Nobody can stay gloomy or mad if in the presence of a Boston Terrier—their naturally sunny and joyous disposition acts as a vitamin to solve the deficiency of happiness in others.

Moving along to another Terrier, let's discuss the Bull Terrier.[2,3] Now at this point, the discerning reader may raise an eyebrow and say that the Bull Terrier was already covered in a previous chapter. To that, I say, that the Bull Terrier is an entirely different dog altogether from the Staffordshire Bull Terrier. The Bull Terrier type that I'm referring to here is the dog breed that serves as a mascot for Target corporation. This is the dog with the long egg-shaped head, and in the days of yore, this breed was bred specifically for baiting bulls. However, the breed is today no longer used as a fighting dog and has instead gone on to become an elegant chum of sorts at home. James Hinks is often credited as being the person responsible for developing the breed.

There is also a miniature version of the Bull Terrier too, which has very similar traits and a zest for life like its bigger counterpart. However, when it comes to the bigger Bull Terrier, one has to be cautious around other dogs, since remnants of the old fighting spirit still remain in the breed. But both

PE(E)KING(ESE) AT JOIE DE VIVRE   105

versions of Bull Terriers are loving toward their own families. Their joie de vivre though is unmistakable, and it's always fun to see a Bull Terrier (of either variety) walking along comically yet looking dapper. This breed is sometimes referred to as the dog with the ultimate personality. And personality is what you get from this breed, along with its insatiable enthusiasm for fun.

Sticking to the Terrier topic (curiously now I feel like I've covered loads of Terriers after first having observed a shortage of them in the book), let me now introduce the Bedlington Terrier[4] to you. This dog has one of the most misleading appearances of all—for all practical purposes, the dog looks like a little lamb. No seriously, take a look at the dog—the Bedlington Terrier absolutely looks like a dainty little lamb. And it displays a wonderful joy for life and is such a happy dog to have around oneself. Indeed, it frolics just like a little lamb itself—however, remember the misleading appearance that I just mentioned two sentences ago. The Bedlington Terrier is one of the fiercest ratters out there. Historically, the Bedlington Terrier was a coalmine ratter and even employed as a pit fighter. This dog breed was also sometimes given the nickname "Gypsy Dog" because of its association with the traveling Romani, who'd often keep these dogs for their brilliant poaching abilities. Of course, the word "Gypsy" is now understood to be derogatory to individuals with Romani ancestry. Subsequently, with the passage of time, nobody refers to the Bedlington Terrier as "Gypsy Dog" any longer. From those working-class origins, the dogs eventually migrated to a more elite class, becoming more popular in manor houses.

Today, the Bedlington Terrier pretty much prances around with the family, expressing lovely joie de vivre. The Bedlington Terrier is one of the happiest-looking dogs out there, and one cannot help but want to cuddle one when you see one. I've met a few Bedlington Terriers in recent times, and it's always been fun meeting them. They are remarkable breeds, and it is a bit unfortunate that not too many people are aware of them. The no-shedding qualities that compel people to go looking for designer breeds are all present in the Bedlington Terrier. So, I'd suggest anyone looking for a non-shedding breed and not wanting one of the hairless varieties, please do consider a Bedlington Terrier. They are remarkable little dogs, which possess a great sense of joy and also help others feel joyous in their presence.

Let's switch tracks here a bit, and go to a dog, that one rarely if ever, thinks of when it comes to joie de vivre. I refer to the chapter's titular breed—the Pekingese[5] (who also made it onto the title of this chapter). This is an ancient breed originating from China and used to be only allowed to be kept by the Emperor or his royal family (indeed, the consequences of a common person stealing one of these dogs were dire). There is an apocryphal legend associated with the Pekingese, and it is that the Buddha shrunk a lion down to a lap dog

106   LEARNING LEADERSHIP FROM DOGS

size, thus resulting in the Pekingese.[6] Another legend speaks of a lion falling in love with a marmoset, and of course, the differing sizes meant that union could never be, till Ah Chu the protector of animals intervened and shrunk the lion's body to a marmoset size, so a lion dog could then be born.[7] Neither of these legends is probably true, but it looks like we'll never really know how the Pekingese was bred and developed since it was all done so long ago, and there aren't any written records of it. The Pekingese was almost lost to posterity, as during the Opium Wars, when the Emperor's summer palace was raided by the invading British troops, the royal family killed all their Pekingese dogs in order to prevent them from falling into their enemies' clutches. But the British troops found five dogs that had somehow escaped being killed, and thus the Pekingese made its way into Western Shores. Ironically, when the Titanic sank, one of the survivors was a Pekingese. So, there's quite a history there, when it comes to the Pekingese.

But keeping aside the history of this ancient breed, let us now talk about its personality. For a royal dog, the Pekingese certainly does possess a distinctive royal gait, and the dog itself appears to harbor a regal appearance. However, the Pekingese is a delightful breed and fully espouses the philosophy of joie de vivre. Pekingese owners often extoll their opinionated dogs and comment on the fun-loving nature of the breed. They can of course be regal and haughty at times, but with their own families, they are highly affectionate and not averse to partaking in a lot of fun activities. It just goes to show that you can be highly regal and yet don't have to go through life like a stuffed frog—there is always time to partake in activities that bring you joy.

Another dog that I must mention here is the Jack Russell Terrier or as it's known in America as the Parson Russell Terrier.[8] The AKC changed the name of Jack Russell Terriers to Parson Russell Terriers in 2004, because they contended that Parson Russell Terriers were long-legged dogs while Jack Russell Terriers were short-legged dogs. Regardless of the leggedness of the dogs though, both varieties of dog exemplify a happy disposition and adherence to a spirit of joie de vivre. Moviegoers will recognize this breed easily since it was really made famous by the character Milo in the Jim Carrey classic movie *The Mask*. Like all Terriers, this breed can be an amazing hunter, but this one was originally employed as a fox-hunting Terrier. Today, of course, the breed is more likely to be a companion dog, but the old skills linger on, and the breed should be supervised if you have smaller pets (like rabbits or hamsters, etc.). These dogs are also happy and energetic dogs—they love life and bring joy to everyone they encounter. Lively and affectionate to the hilt, are these Parson Russell (or if you prefer, Jack Russell) Terriers.

At this point, while I could rattle along with the remaining dogs I plan to cover in this chapter, I figure it would be judicious to have a section that talks a bit more descriptively about why exactly joie de vivre is an important attitude for leaders to possess.

Why Possess Joie De Vivre?

While I have discussed what joie de vivre is and also discussed several dog breeds that exemplify the attitude, I think it would also be judicious to explain a bit more why that attitude is a highly recommended one for leaders to espouse. Essentially, as I explained in the very beginning, joie de vivre has to do with happiness, overall happiness. People who espouse it tend to be happy in general, and happiness comes with a whole host of positive benefits.[9] If a person tends to be a happy individual, they tend to be healthier both mentally and physically. Happy individuals (and leaders of course) tend not to be highly stressed out, and are able to live balanced lives[10]—instead of getting harried and frantic, and increasing stress for themselves and all and sundry.

I knew this one CEO who was a highly stressed-out individual—one of his habits was to shout at his employees whenever he was stressed out, which was a perennial state of affairs. He was judged as being perennially grumpy, and due to a result, he suffered more than three heart attacks, which he was lucky didn't prove to be fatal heart attacks. The poor man finally retired, and after his retirement, I happened to meet him—he seemed like a completely different individual altogether. He had discovered joie de vivre after all, even if much later, and he in fact, mused that if he had that spirit when he was the CEO, perhaps his leadership tenure wouldn't have been quite so adversarial to his health or image. On the flip side, another CFO turned CEO I know quite well was the polar opposite of this other leader. He was always joyous at work and in his own personal life, and his employees loved working with him, due to the happiness that radiated from him. He truly lived and espoused joie de vivre to the maximum, and even now, after retirement, he is enjoying a lovely fulfilling life, and still giving back to the community.

While misery is contagious, happiness is too—we've all heard the old chestnut saying about happy cows producing more milk. When it comes to leaders, one could modify that to read as happy leaders produce happier employees.[11] I must say here that I don't mean fake happiness—I am referring to true or authentic happiness. That's why I think we really can learn so much from dogs because most of what dogs express and display is authentic. When they show joy, that is genuine joy—they are not acting happy, they truly are happy. That true happiness or true joy is what I am referring to when I refer

108 LEARNING LEADERSHIP FROM DOGS

to joie de vivre. That is what we ought to be learning from dogs. Alright, so let's get to discussing more dogs here, that I think exemplify this spirit of joy.

More Dogs Who Exemplify Joie De Vivre

Now, let's gallop along, and leave the world of Terriers for a bit, to go seeking for some hounds again. To be precise, the Scottish Deerhound[12] is what I have in mind here. Sometimes, people mistake the Deerhound with the Wolfhound, but there are significant differences between the two. For starters, the Deerhound is a lot slenderer than the Wolfhounds are—of course, they both are sight hounds and equally majestic. The Deerhound was bred as a royal dog and used to course the large red deer found in Scotland. Today of course, we don't see the Deerhound being used for hunting deer as much, although we do see a lot of nonroyals having Deerhounds at home nowadays. This dog is a beautiful lovely spirited being and a joy to share one's life with. The Deerhound is polite as most hounds tend to be, and it has an amazing attitude to life. The Scottish Deerhound embraces long walks and runs, but is also equally at ease napping on a sofa. This easygoing attitude and affectionate disposition are both attributes that demonstrate the Deerhound's penchant for joie de vivre. The only thing potential Deerhound owners should know is that like all coursing hounds, they cannot resist chasing small animals that run past. So, if you have a cat or a smaller dog, the Deerhound will chase the small animal, which may not be pleasant tidings for the smaller animal.

Let's discuss two Portuguese dogs next—the first is the Portuguese Water Dog,[13] and the other is the Portuguese Podengo.[14] The Portuguese Water Dog became very popular in the United States after President Barack Obama got one and then another for his daughters. This is another intelligent and easy-to-train dog, and while it has a past as a fisherman's helper, most people who have one nowadays really have no fishing background. This is yet another happy dog that bounces about in delight and has high intelligence combined with high curiosity levels. But either way, anyone in proximity to a Portuguese Water Dog cannot but fail to feel happy, and that's an important takeaway.

Coming to the Portuguese Podengo, there are three sizes of this particular breed—small, medium, and large. It is relatively new in terms of being recognized by the AKC, but of course, it's been well known for a while in Portugal. The breed is considered a no-frills and primitive breed. The word primitive does not mean anything derogatory, all that it signals is that the dog has not been affected by fashion fads etc., and pretty much looks similar to how it looked in the past. This is in contrast to other breeds, where fashion fads have changed breeds entirely to make them look completely different. But

PE(E)KING(ESE) AT JOIE DE VIVRE 109

anyhow, the Podengo is another happy and alert breed, which is always happy to play with their owners and family members. They are equally at home coursing or taking part in barn hunts. In their native Portugal, depending on the size, they are used to hunt boar or rabbit. This is a fun breed to have as a pet, and its owners and fanciers will swear by its ability to inspire happiness through its attitude and demeanor.

From sunny Portugal, let us cast our eyes to relatively rainier Belgium, by discussing the Brussels Griffon.[15] As the name suggests, this amusing dog hails from Brussels and is a small dog, usually never exceeding 15 pounds in weight. The Brussels Griffon doesn't seem to realize that it is a small dog though—it has enough personality for a whole platoon of dogs. Many have pointed out that the Brussels Griffon resembles a grizzly philosopher about to embark on a brainy soliloquy, but despite that academic air about it, the dog has a lovely notion of joie de vivre. The dog is playful and alertly energetic, although its small size does preclude it from engaging in too much horseplay with younger children. But it has an indubitable air of joy about it, and that joy transfers easily to those in its vicinity.

Another breed which I simply cannot fail to include in this August list of happy and joyous breeds is the Corgi. While both the Pembroke Welsh[16] and Cardigan Welsh Corgis[17] have similarities in personality and dispositions, the Cardigans do tend to be slightly more serious. The Pembroke Welsh Corgis in contrast are a lot more outgoing and possibly more fun-loving. They're both happy dogs though, although in my experience, I have noticed that the Pembrokes really love hanging out with kids. This one time at the local dog park, my younger son, myself, and Fiona met a friendly happy Corgi named Milo, who hung out with us the entire time we were there. We ended up making friends with the owners of Milo, and it was quite a fun happy outing. Queen Elizabeth was always a Pembroke Welsh Corgi aficionado and was quite devoted to Corgis. This is yet another breed that fully espouses the principle of joie de vivre—if you're on Instagram, you'll probably recognize the meme which uses a happy Corgi seemingly smirking at an inside joke. That meme seems so apt to me because it really does capture the essence of a Pembroke Welsh Corgi's jubilant joy. If only we could experience a fraction of that authentic joy ourselves […].

The final dog I'll be covering in this chapter is probably known to all Disney-watching audiences across the world. Yes, the Dalmatian[18] is the dog which will be discussed now. *101 Dalmatians* was a huge sensation across the globe, and the dog was always fairly popular prior to that movie, but the movie really ramped up the popularity of the breed sky-high. One of my best friends Venkat had a lovely Dalmatian named Rover, who was such a delightful happy dog. Joyous and thrilled to be living life and

110   LEARNING LEADERSHIP FROM DOGS

enjoying it to the fullest extent. The origins of this breed are a bit shrouded in inscrutability, but most people agree that the Dalmatia area around the Adriatic Sea is probably the area where the breed as we know it was developed. The Dalmatian was also known as a Fireman's dog because they would often run alongside the fire engines (that association started during the time when horses propelled fire engines). And it was also known as a Coach Dog—the function which it performed was to guard the horses and the coach itself, when the coachman was away on duty or a break. Dalmatians have wonderful dispositions and are dignified dogs through and through. They live life joyfully and also help their owners and family members find plenty of joy in the process.

How Do You Become Joyful?

Now we've read about so many dogs, and learned about what makes them tick, and we've also learned why it is important to possess a sense of joie de vivre. But the question remains, how do we do that? If we don't have a naturally joyous personality, how do we even begin to develop it? One of the biggest reasons for a total lack of joy is disconnectedness, which can be likened to a sense of anomie. This was a phenomenon studied by Emile Durkheim, which referred to a sense of normlessness.[19] That sort of normlessness really does contribute to a lack of joy. That suggests that one way to avoid feeling a disconnect from one's environment is to get out into one's environment and explore it fully. Walk around in your neighborhood, or your office building, etc. Try and make connections, and you'll soon discover an uptick in your happiness levels. And of course, apart from making new connections, reach out and reconnect with the people you already do know. It will be beneficial for you to do that.

Another way to improve your sense of joie de vivre is to deliberately seek out and engage in activities you truly like. Carve out a little bit of time to do things outside of work—the joyous CEO I mentioned a little while ago is a big fishing enthusiast. One of the ways he would recharge himself and continue to stay healthy was to go fishing. There is always a benefit to carving out time for yourself—yes, there is limited time in one's life, but budget for some time for yourself. That bit of time for yourself will handsomely pay off in the long term for you and your health.

Another way to improve your own level of happiness is to understand yourself better—gain some or improve your self-awareness to be able to figure out what it is that makes you happy. Different people have differing tastes, and there is no universal answer to this question, is there? Sometimes it may involve making changes in your life, be they personal or life or professional changes. That may be what it takes to get you to embrace this spirit of joie de vivre. All of the various dogs I've discussed here in this chapter offer lessons on how we can improve our own sense and spirit of joie de vivre. Just like the various dog breeds know what they like, we need to know what we like, and we need to make sure that we get to do what we enjoy doing. In the end, material riches alone aren't what will keep us happy—they may work in the short term, but long term, will require a more judicious understanding of ourselves.

Summary

In this chapter, I discuss the concept of happiness or joie de vivre and outline why it is important for individuals and leaders to have a spirit of joie de vivre. There are loads of positive outcomes by embracing joie de vivre. I have discussed dog breeds like the Boston Terrier, Bull Terrier, Pekingese, Scottish Deerhound, Pembroke Welsh Corgi, and Dalmatian among others, in the context of joie de vivre. I have also discussed why leaders should embrace that spirit, as well as how they can begin to do so. In Chapter 11, I will be discussing the topic of resilience, and discuss and describe several dog breeds that exemplify resilience.

Boston Terrier   Bull Terrier

Bedlington Terrier   Pekingese

112 LEARNING LEADERSHIP FROM DOGS

Parsons Russell Terrier

Portuguese Water Dog

Portuguese Podengo

Scottish Deerhound

Pembroke Welsh Corgi

Cardigan Welsh Corgi

Brussels Griffon

Dalmatian

References

1 https://www.akc.org/dog-breeds/boston-terrier/.
2 https://www.akc.org/dog-breeds/bull-terrier/.
3 https://www.thekennelclub.org.uk/search/breeds-a-to-z/breeds/terrier/bull-terrier/.
4 https://www.thekennelclub.org.uk/search/breeds-a-to-z/breeds/terrier/bedlington-terrier/.
5 https://www.akc.org/dog-breeds/pekingese/.
6 https://www.akc.org/expert-advice/dog-breeds/ancient-mysterious-lost-legends-imperial-pekingese/.
7 https://moderndogmagazine.com/articles/breeds/the-pekingese/.
8 https://www.akc.org/dog-breeds/parson-russell-terrier/.
9 Andrews, C. (2006). *Slow is Beautiful: New Visions of Community, Leisure, and Joie De Vivre.* Gabriola Island, Canada: New Society Publishers.
10 Christensen, M. (2017). Healthy individuals in healthy organizations: The happy productive worker hypothesis. *The Positive Side of Occupational Health Psychology,* 155–169.
11 Fiset, J., & Boies, K. (2019). Positively vivid visions: Making followers feel capable and happy. *Human Relations,* 72(10), 1651–1670.
12 https://www.thekennelclub.org.uk/search/breeds-a-to-z/breeds/hound/deerhound/.
13 https://www.akc.org/dog-breeds/portuguese-water-dog/.
14 https://www.thekennelclub.org.uk/search/breeds-a-to-z/breeds/hound/portuguese-podengo/.
15 https://www.akc.org/dog-breeds/brussels-griffon/.
16 https://www.akc.org/dog-breeds/pembroke-welsh-corgi/.
17 https://www.akc.org/dog-breeds/cardigan-welsh-corgi/.
18 https://www.akc.org/dog-breeds/dalmatian/.
19 Marks, S. R. (1974). Durkheim's theory of anomie. *American Journal of Sociology,* 80(2), 329–363.

Chapter 11

RIDGE(ING) BACK TO RESILIENCE

Resilience is a word and an attribute that is increasingly becoming more and more familiar in the world of leadership. After all, one cannot be expected to always win in every situation. There are plenty of times when one ends up snatching a loss from the jaws of victory—I know the expression probably seems a little lopsided to most readers, but I've always found it deliciously ironic. In a situation of failure, most people would be reasonably expected to be rather devastated. The ability to bounce back from failure is what resilience is all about. If one has to define resilience, then usually the definition involves the ability to face or respond to a failure or a drawback of some kind. Resilience could be on a continuum of course—for instance, a person may be resilient in one area, but less so in another area. However, from a leadership perspective, resilience is often thought to be one of the components of psychological capital or PsyCap[1] as it is popularly acronymized as.

PsyCap basically refers to the internal resources a person has in order to be able to manage difficult or turbulent situations. It consists of four components, namely hope, efficacy, resilience, and optimism.[1-4] As you can see, each component of it helps people tackle tough times. For instance, a person definitely needs a healthy dose of optimism and hope when facing tough times, and similarly needs to be confident in one's own ability to eventually be successful. The resilience piece specifically deals with how a person can deal with and overcome challenging or stressful circumstances, and still be able to forge forward.

Dogs are among nature's most resilient animals, and many-a-dog has displayed amazing tenacity and the ability to bounce back from really awful and harrowing situations. That ability to bounce back from emotionally or physically draining activities and incidents is what resilience is all about. Although, one could make the case, that possessing high levels of overall psychological capital is an essential recipe for being able to bounce back from failure and go on to a successful outcome. There are many ways of looking at resilience, but if we stick to the Luthans approach, it becomes a lot easier to comprehend it. So, in this chapter, I'm going to be loosely basing

116 LEARNING LEADERSHIP FROM DOGS

the explanation of resilience around Fred Luthans concept of psychological capital or PsyCap.

As always, I will feature and discuss several dog breeds in this chapter, and these dogs will be breeds that I believe make for great poster children of resilience. Most dogs are naturally gifted with ample quantities of resilience, but there are some breeds which I think really exemplify resilience. I will be describing those dogs here and also will discuss how leaders can increase their own reservoirs of resilience. So, let's start off with the dogs right away then—in this chapter, I think we will have the maximum number of dogs being discussed as when compared with other chapters. There's only one more chapter left, so let's continue to be resilient and forge on ahead.

Some Dogs Which Exemplify Resilience

There are a variety of dogs out there, many of which we've already read about in the duration of this book. When it comes to resilience, for me, the dog that first comes to mind is the lithe Greyhound.[5] This dog's origins probably trace back to ancient Egypt, but the modern version of the breed is likely from England. DNA results suggest that an ancient now-extinct breed called the Vertragus is probably one of the ancestors of the Greyhound. The Greyhound is probably one of the oldest coursing hounds and is perfectly suited to high-speed pursuits (especially of rabbits and hares). It has one of the most aerodynamic skull shapes, and amazing shock-absorbing feet pads, which help it achieve success in high-speed pursuits.

This is the fastest dog breed out there (it achieves speeds of up to 45 miles per hour), and as a direct result of this Hermes-like speed, the Greyhound was used in the "sport" of dog racing. Inevitably though, when the craze for dog racing receded, there were so many retired racers who were now left adrift without any occupation. You'll see a lot of Greyhound rescues now, across the US. This is a direct result of many states banning dog racing, because of the dangers from that industry toward Greyhounds. And of course, a lot of Greyhound racing track places went out of business due to dwindling income. Many of the Greyhound owners and handlers would simply discard their retired Greyhounds after they were no longer competitive on the track. Quite sad for that to happen, but the heartening thing is that despite all those troubles, the Greyhound continues to display a great deal of resilience. They adjust quickly from being neglected and often cruelly treated racers to being happy contented family pets. I've met several Greyhounds in the past few years, and they've all been rescued racing dogs. The common trait they all have is their gentleness, and their ability to adjust to being loved pets from a somewhat hard life as a harried racing dog. The Greyhound is definitely

RIDGE(ING) BACK TO RESILIENCE 117

a dog we can all learn resilience from—sometimes, in life, we may need to possess a modicum of resilience, and taking our cues from the Greyhound would do us a world of good.

A distant relative of the Greyhound, but relatively unknown outside India is the beautiful Rampur Greyhound.[6] This is a rather rare dog even in its native country of origin, and was developed by the Nawab of Rampur. The Rampur Greyhound is a dog which was bred from Greyhounds and Afghan Hounds and is a masterful coursing hound. The Nawab and later royals also used the Rampur Greyhound for hunting jackal and boar. This is another dog that is super resilient, and tales abound of times when these dogs would run doggedly until a hunting trip or expedition was finally successful. Another tireless and very resilient breed, this. It is a bit of a pity that the breed is so rare nowadays—it is a strikingly handsome dog, and I wish more people knew about it. Hopefully, the resilience of this breed will not be lost to future generations, but sadly, without proper steps taken, it may be a sign of things to come.

Sticking to India for a bit, another beautiful and resilient breed that comes to my mind is the Mudhol Hound.[7] This dog is a native breed from a place called Mudhol Taluk in the state of Karnataka in India. This breed is also called the Caravan Hound, but over the past decade or so, the Mudhol name has become the preferred one. This dog is probably one of the most popular Indian local breeds, and you are more likely to see families with Indian breeds with the Mudhol Hound than any other Indian native breed. In appearance, the dog looks like a Greyhound of sorts and is equally resilient. The Indian Army is now looking into seeing whether the Mudhol Hound can be used for border protection duties. This is partly being done due to the extreme resilience which is displayed by the Mudhol Hound, and partly because of the Indian government's desire to review and popularize Indian local breeds.

Switching gears, a little back, let's saunter along to the UK (and US too, one must add) to mention another really vulnerable breed, the Fox Hound. You have two varieties of this breed, one is the English Foxhound,[8] and the other, the American Fox Hound.[9] The main difference appears to be that the American variety is longer and a bit thinner than its English counterpart. Both breeds are sadly vulnerable, with the English variety being especially vulnerable. This is another determined dog which displays a lot of resilience and is a determined hunting hound. The American Fox Hound is the official state dog of Virginia, and while the dog is one of the sweetest kinds of dogs out there as a family member, it can be incredibly resilient and determined. Some Foxhound owners have claimed that their dogs never give up on a hunt, and are always game to trying again even after an unsuccessful hunt. Now that's resilience in a nutshell!

118 LEARNING LEADERSHIP FROM DOGS

Sticking to sight hounds, let's discuss another relatively unknown long-legged beauty, the elegant Azawakh.[10] This dog breed originally hails from the region between the Sahara and the Sahel zones, which includes countries like Burkina Faso, Mali, and Niger. This dog was closely associated with the Tuareg nomadic people. It was traditionally called the "idii n' illeli," which literally means sighthound of the free people. This dog may look like a slender delicate being, but is one of the most resilient hunters of all dogs. The Azawakh has the ability to go miles and miles chasing after gazelles in the desert, and the rough terrain in the desert areas poses no trouble at all to these dogs. Today of course, they are equally at home being house pets, but their resilience remains intact. Another breed which looks similar but hails from North Africa, and was closely connected with the Bedouin and Berber people, is the Sloughi.[11] That dog too is an incredibly resilient and courageous dog, which quite represents resilience in all its glory.

I was going to go into the discussion about how do we increase resilience ourselves but figured that I may as well talk about one more sighthound, from the Middle East this time. I am talking about the pretty as a picture of Saluki.[12] This is another incredibly courageous and resilient hunting dog and used for gazelle hunting as well as hare. They are amazingly adaptable and able to live and hunt in a variety of climates. Despite their slight look, they are strong dogs and show great determination. In previous eras, in the Middle East, these dogs were never sold—instead, they were gifted to people as a symbol of respect. Fortunately, now there are plenty of breeders around that you can procure a Saluki puppy from for yourself. They make dignified and loyal pets and are affectionate with their families yet aloof with strangers.

Now I'm going to segue a bit away from dogs and talk about ways by which we ourselves can improve our resilience levels, and become better and more resilient leaders. After that, another section on more examples of resilient dogs would be a befitting segue.

How to Improve Your Own Resilience

There are several ways to improve or increase your own sense of resiliency. The first is believe it or not getting used to taking risk. Think about it, if you don't ever take any risks, you run the risk (ha ha) of never failing. While never failing at anything may sound like a great idea, it doesn't do a whole lot of good for a person. By being extremely risk averse, one ends up foregoing the opportunity to grow. One can only grow reasonably by taking reasonable risks—think of it in terms of exercising. Only by adding more weights and resistance levels to your exercise routine, can you begin to see any sort of forward momentum. One does need to ensure that the weights or resistance

RIDGE(ING) BACK TO RESILIENCE

levels aren't dangerous in terms of causing incalculable injuries. But judicious risk is what keeps us going forward and growing.

Again, the definition of risk is variable—one person's definition of risky may be a walk in the park for another person, and one person's walk in the park may be risk central for the other. Another leader I know who was a long-tenured CEO in a Fortune 500 company often uses the skydiving context to explain risk tolerance. He says that skydiving may be horribly risky for some, but for others, it may not even invite a single gasp of anxiety. It goes to show that risk is variable, but the beauty of that variability is that there are multiple ways for us all to become more resilient. Two ways about it—if you take on a judicious risk, and it fails, you can still bounce back and eventually wrest victory from the jaws of defeat (instead of the ironic opposite). And if you somehow make the risk pay off, then hey, nothing to complain about, is there?

The whole point about being resilient is that one needs to understand that failure is a part and parcel of life, and it's not the failure that matters, it's whether or not we can shrug it off and rise up and strive for success again. Personally speaking, I have to publish articles in journals, and that is an exercise in frustration. But I do my best to continue on even while knowing that the overall acceptance rates across journals is a dismal low single-digit number (especially in the better-quality and better-ranked journals). It takes months and sometimes years before your work gets accepted by journal editors, who are themselves facing similar issues. Some people do give up—they stop submitting articles to journals, which only means that eventually, they can never get back into the publishing game. One really needs to be resilient, in order to achieve a modicum of success. One should always remember to be hopeful and develop a thick skin because that's what still striving for success even after multiple failures does to us.

This is exactly the kind of attitude that leaders need to embrace—if a project or a pet initiative fails, they shouldn't just throw in the towel. Shrug it off and try again. We all remember the old legend about the Scottish King, King Bruce and the spider,[13] where the embattled king observes the spider in the cave weaving a web. The spider tries, tries, and tries again, and the king, who was in hiding in the cave at that moment, learns a lesson about resiliency. While it may seem like a child's tale, it actually offers a powerful metaphor to children and adults alike. When plans fail, one must go back to the drawing board, and edit or modify, and try again.

Additionally, it is the responsibility of leaders to bring forth a climate of resilience throughout their organization. One way to do that is to remove the fear of failure from their followers—if a follower fears the leader's reaction to failure, that is not a healthy climate to cultivate. This is the perfect time to remember a quote by Claire Cook who said that if plan A doesn't work,

120 LEARNING LEADERSHIP FROM DOGS

there are still twenty-five more letters in the alphabet. One could modify this to add that there are eight billion (at least) combinations of these letters. So, if a follower fails, as long as that person learns from the failure, the leader shouldn't be taking punitive measures against the employee. Once punitive measures start being taken, all that will happen is that the followers will hide failures, or never own up to their own failures, and instead scapegoat others.

Of course, it would be foolish to keep trying for something when the outcome is impossible—but it is equally foolish to stop trying just because the last outcome was unsuccessful. As an example of the former case, let us say that there's an entrance exam you're trying to clear, and there's an age limit that is enforced—if you exceed that age limit, then you're just not going to clear the exam, no matter what you do. You'll need a TARDIS to go back in time or something; that's the kind of impossible situation I'm referring to. If there is hope for success, then you must try again with your best effort. That is what resilience is all about.

So, you've got to embrace risk and forge ahead even if you encounter failure. Success comes to those who don't give up and self-select themselves out. That is one of the biggest reasons why some people remain chronically underemployed or unemployed—they give up! If you give up, you'll never get that job you didn't apply for—but if you apply for it, there's a small chance of that coming through. Mental bulwarking is the order of the day when one wants to start building up resilience—learn to start getting used to small failures and bouncing back from those, before moving on to learning to bounce back from bigger failures. All these failures and your responses to them are what will increase your mental fortitude and make you more resilient. Mentally prepare yourself for the contingency of failure, be ready to shake it off, and continue striving for success. Retaining hope is definitely a key component to making a person resilient—so never lose sight of hope. Now, let's move back to the world of dogs, to learn more about some more resilient breeds of dogs.

Some More Resilient Breeds of Dogs

Let me introduce the dog that's responsible for the title of this particular chapter—the Rhodesian Ridgeback.[14] The dog originally originates from South Africa, and the "ridge" in its name refers to the backward-growing hair which is found on its back. The original dog involved a mix of several local African dogs with European dogs such as Greyhounds and Terriers. The local breed infusion helped inure the dog against local pests like the Tsetse fly. These dogs excel at resilience and are amazingly fearless—they were used in the hunting of lions and fending off of baboons. A pack of Ridgebacks could track and keep lions at bay, while the hunter was getting ready to shoot the lion with a gun. They were reputed to be doggedly determined in the pursuit and could run after and keep the quarry at bay for a long time, across terrains. The first breeder in the US was Hollywood actor Errol Flynn,[15] although his kennel's bloodline is now extinct. The Rhodesian Ridgeback is one of South Africa's the most legendary breeds and is easily recognized thanks to its iconic ridge. The breed is definitely one of a kind, and incredibly brave and resilient. Today, they aren't used to hunt lions anymore, but they are used in other countries to hunt mountain lions and bears.

Another dog that fits the profile to be featured from a resilience point of view is the Bullmastiff.[16] This dog was developed by English gamekeepers in the nineteenth century, as a direct response to poaching. They wanted a dog that was big enough yet lithe enough to be able to tackle a poacher, but not maul the poacher. Bullmastiffs were raised and trained to be able to hold the poacher without harming the poacher, but holding the poacher in such a way that the poacher had zero chances of escaping. Bullmastiffs are basically a mix of Bulldogs and Mastiffs, and the optimal magic ratio for size and temperament was 60% Mastiff and 40% Bulldog. Of course, they kept refining the breed till they got the magic ratio of 60–40, but once they got it, they found that the Bullmastiff was perfect as an anti-poaching deterrent. The dogs were big enough yet gentle enough not to maul the poacher up. Additionally, they were resilient enough not to let failure deter them, and their reliability in terms of temperament was legendary. Now though, it seems that there is a bit of a loss of luster in that stellar reputation, but regardless, it still continues to be a resilient dog. If I were a poacher (not that I would be one), the last dog I'd want to be confronted by at night would be a big giant 130-pound dog.

I just realized that all of the dogs I've covered so far in this chapter have been big dogs or at least medium-sized dogs, so here's to an extremely resilient little dog, namely the Scottish Terrier.[17] I fell in love with this breed thanks to the amazing tales of Buster the Scottish Terrier from Enid Blyton's *Five Find-Outers* series. This breed is a plucky and filled to the gills with a personality kind of dog. They were bred to be fierce vermin hunters, and would not back down from the task, no matter what. If the rats got going, the Scottish Terrier would ensure that they stay gone. It was (and continues to be) a super resilient breed. Another little dog that can be really resilient is the West Highland White Terrier.[18] This dog was intentionally bred to be white because the red Cairn Terrier could be mistaken for a fox and accidentally shot (as was the case for Colonel Malcolm, who then decided to breed all White Terriers, which became the Westie we know today). The West Highland White Terrier is another super resilient breed, which was bred to be able to jump onto rocks and crawl and squeeze through small crevices to pursue foxes. This dog does not back

122   LEARNING LEADERSHIP FROM DOGS

away from a confrontation with its quarry even if a previous encounter wasn't successful. It certainly seems to highlight resilience, doesn't it?

Let's talk about gundogs again—I did discuss the various Setters in the past, but I'm going to now discuss two special gundogs—the Hungarian Vizsla[19] and the Weimaraner.[20] Both of these dogs have such high energy that if you end up owning one of them, you will have to become high energy yourself, even if you're not. Both dogs are beautiful with distinguishable colored coats and brilliant stamina. These dogs can work all day in any kind of condition, be it wet or hot or windy or cold, etc. These two breeds are among the most resilient gundogs of all, which is why they are so popular with the sporting and birding dog owners. The Hungarian Vizsla was a dog, which was a favorite of the Hungarian aristocrats, who called the breed as a gift from the gods. Ditto for the Weimaraner, which was kept by the nobility at the German Court of Weimar. Today of course, even people from non-nobility backgrounds can still keep these two breeds and marvel at being able to keep such beautiful and high-energy dogs. If you keep one of these two dog breeds and are a conscientious person, you will naturally become quite fit, because of all of the exercise you'll be needing to give these dogs.

At this point, I'd like to revisit three dogs, that I alluded to back in Chapter 6 when I discussed the Grand Bleu de Gascogne. Remember reading about how the Grand Bleu de Gascogne dogs simply couldn't figure out how to hunt raccoons when the latter went climbing up trees. As a result, the Coonhound ended up getting bred from the Grand Bleu and other breeds. The resultant lot of Coonhounds which includes the Black and Tan Coonhound,[21] the Bluetick Coonhound,[22] the Redbone Coonhound,[23] the American English Coonhound,[24] and Treeing Walker Coonhound[25] are four distinctive looking hounds, but all of them share the attribute of resilience. These various Coonhounds differ in terms of size, color, and ancestry (e.g., the American English Coonhound has Foxhound ancestry). All these Coonhounds are unbelievably resilient and tenacious when it comes to chasing after their raccoon prey. All these dogs have beautiful and sonorous voices, which you can hear across distances. So, if you live in a quiet neighborhood, it won't be too quiet much longer, since the Coonhound baying will resonate across the neighborhood, and everyone will know. All of these dogs are brilliantly resilient, and will not rest until their quarry has been vanquished. If the quarry somehow escapes one day, these dogs will not hang their boots the next day, but instead head back again for another chance to get their prey. However, even if you're not a hunting person, these Coonhounds are equally at home snoozing on your couch, like all hound dogs love.

Another dog this time hailing from Louisiana is the Catahoula Leopard Dog,[26] which is a really striking-looking dog. This breed has the most

RIDGE(ING) BACK TO RESILIENCE

amazing herding quality—they create a "canine fence" inside which the herd gets directed by the actual shepherd or farmer. Very unique, this, and sets the Catahoula Leopard Dog apart from other herding breeds. The Leopard in its name refers to the multicolored spotted coat—when I was younger, I'd always imagine how a dog from Louisiana was named after a leopard when there were no leopards in the US. Ah well, now I know, and now you know too. This breed is another tenacious breed that never gives up—it excels at both herding and hunting, which is quite rare to see in a dog. It can work across terrain types and is high on its resilience levels.

The final dog breed that I'm going to talk about in this chapter is the Tibetan Mastiff.[27] There was a time about a decade ago when these Mastiffs were all the rage across China. The most expensive dog in the world at one point in time, was a Tibetan Mastiff from China, which was sold for two million USD, back in 2014. Today, however, the breed is out of fashion, and as a result, many Tibetan Mastiffs have been abandoned by their owners, and now roam around the Tibetan plateau, resulting in aggressive behavior toward all they encounter there.[28] What a shame, isn't it? The dog is one of the most powerful guarding dogs of all and can be quite fierce and fearsome. These dogs are naturally territorial—I remember a neighbor of one of my uncles had a Tibetan Mastiff, which was horribly fearsome. I wouldn't want to be the burglar or robber who picks a house guarded by a Tibetan Mastiff as a potential place to go rob. This breed is superbly resilient too, as we can clearly see, with the incidents on the Tibetan plateau. Hopefully, all the dogs who've been abandoned by their owners can be rehomed safely with other families. In terms of resiliency, this breed is brilliant at protecting livestock as well as in protecting monasteries in its native Tibet, and with its size and temperament, it's no mystery as to why that is the case.

Well, I don't think I should discuss any more dog breeds in this chapter, as there's been a pretty robust discussion of plenty of breeds thus far. I do hope you realize the resilience factor emanating from these various breeds too.

Summary

In this chapter, I discuss the concept of resilience and outline why it is important for individuals and leaders to have an attitude for and appetite for resilience. I have discussed dog breeds like the Greyhound, Saluki, Tibetan Mastiff, Scottish Terrier, and Mudhol Hound, among others, in the context of resilience. I have also discussed how leaders could improve their own resilience levels. In Chapter 12, I will be pretty much offering a summary of the book—it's time to bring this book to an end in Chapter 12. See you at the conclusion next chapter, that is, chapter 12.

124 LEARNING LEADERSHIP FROM DOGS

Greyhound Rampur Hound

Mudhol Hound Fox Hound

Azawakh Sloughi

Saluki Rhodesian Ridgeback

RIDGE(ING) BACK TO RESILIENCE 125

West Highland White Terrier

Weimaraner

Scottish Terrier

Bullmastiff

Hungarian Vizsla

Walker Treeing Coonhound

Bluetick Coonhound

Black and Tan Coonhound

Redbone Coonhound

American English Coonhound

Tibetan Mastiff

Catahoula Leopard Dog

References

1. Luthans, F., & Youssef-Morgan, C. M. (2017). Psychological capital: An evidence-based positive approach. *Annual Review of Organizational Psychology and Organizational Behavior*, 4, 339–366.
2. Luthans, F., Avey, J. B., Avolio, B. J., Norman, S. M., & Combs, G. M. (2006). Psychological capital development: toward a micro-intervention. *Journal of Organizational Behavior*, 27(3), 387–393.
3. Sweetman, D., Luthans, F., Avey, J. B., & Luthans, B. C. (2011). Relationship between positive psychological capital and creative performance. *Canadian Journal of Administrative Sciences*, 28(1), 4–13.
4. Luthans, F., Avey, J. B., Avolio, B. J., & Peterson, S. J. (2010). The development and resulting performance impact of positive psychological capital. *Human Resource Development Quarterly*, 21(1), 41–67.
5. https://www.akc.org/dog-breeds/greyhound/.
6. https://discover.hubpages.com/animals/The-Royal-Dogs-of-India.
7. https://www.dogsglobal.com/breeds/mudhol-hound.
8. https://www.thekennelclub.org.uk/search/breeds-a-to-z/breeds/hound/foxhound/.
9. https://www.akc.org/dog-breeds/american-foxhound/.
10. https://www.akc.org/dog-breeds/azawakh/.
11. https://www.akc.org/dog-breeds/sloughi/.
12. https://www.akc.org/dog-breeds/saluki/.
13. https://hiddenscotland.co/bruce-the-spider-in-kings-cave/.

RIDGE(ING) BACK TO RESILIENCE — 127

14 https://www.akc.org/dog-breeds/rhodesian-ridgeback/.
15 https://nationalpurebreddogday.com/the-swashbuckling-rhodesian-ridgeback/.
16 https://www.thekennelclub.org.uk/search/breeds-a-to-z/breeds/working/bullmastiff.
17 https://www.thekennelclub.org.uk/search/breeds-a-to-z/breeds/terrier/scottish-terrier/.
18 https://www.thekennelclub.org.uk/search/breeds-a-to-z/breeds/terrier/west-highland-white-terrier/.
19 https://www.akc.org/dog-breeds/vizsla/.
20 https://www.akc.org/dog-breeds/weimaraner/.
21 https://www.akc.org/dog-breeds/black-and-tan-coonhound/.
22 https://www.akc.org/dog-breeds/bluetick-coonhound/.
23 https://www.akc.org/dog-breeds/redbone-coonhound/.
24 https://www.akc.org/dog-breeds/american-english-coonhound/.
25 https://www.akc.org/dog-breeds/treeing-walker-coonhound/.
26 https://www.akc.org/dog-breeds/catahoula-leopard-dog/.
27 https://www.akc.org/dog-breeds/tibetan-mastiff/.
28 https://www.scmp.com/lifestyle/family-relationships/article/3114112/tibetan-mastiff-dogs-ravaging-wildlife-mauling.

Chapter 12

SETTER(ING) DOWN TO A CONCLUSION

The end is almost nigh [...] well, at least the end of this book is almost near, to be precise. Here, we are finally at the final chapter of this particular volume. It was certainly a lot of fun for me to write this book, as I was able to dive somewhat deep into the world of dogs, which is a world I've been an avid fan of since I was a kid. I must have read hundreds of books on dogs and various dog breeds and attended several dog shows in both India as well as the US. And I plan to continue attending some more shows in the days to come, I have also gone on short trips and visits to meet with several dog breeders—it's always fun to go meet a new or unique breed. In short, I really do love dogs—they are such wonderful beings and companions, that life is truly unfathomable without them.

The whole idea behind this book was to write about certain qualities that I believe are qualities leaders ought to have, in order to be exemplary and effective leaders. I attempt to show you how we can learn about those qualities by learning about dogs. I have essentially described various dog breeds and attempted to showcase how they embody the qualities that I consider essential for leaders. Through the various chapters in the book, I have endeavored to introduce you (i.e., the swashbuckling reader) to a variety of dog breeds, some of which you may have already known about, but I bet there are many breeds in here, which you've never heard about, and now after reading the book, you have. As I've alluded to in several places in the book, many dog breeds actually would have fit into multiple chapters throughout the book, but I intentionally wanted to focus on unique breeds per chapter, instead of using the same breeds throughout. Otherwise, honestly, I could have probably written the whole book with just seven dog breeds, that is, the titular five and maybe a Shepherd or a Retriever to round up a magnificent seven. But I also want this book to help people learn about the many wonderful dog breeds out there in the world—there are loads more that I simply couldn't even begin to cover in the book. There are so many more dog breeds that I would have loved to have written about, but then it ran the risk of the book becoming Tolstoyian in

130   LEARNING LEADERSHIP FROM DOGS

length, which would have been problematic, to say the least (just imagine the shipping charges for a hardcover book that's a 1000-pages long). My sincere apologies to anyone who feels a bit miffed that their favorite dog breed wasn't featured in any of the chapters—it wasn't intentional, I assure you.

This chapter is sort of similar to a conclusion section that one has in a research article, where the author(s) point out what the rest of the treatise covers. I will be doing something similar here to discuss how individuals can take these various concepts discussed in the book and improve their own leadership skills. In the end, there are many qualities that are indelibly associated with effectiveness, as I've laid out in the past eleven chapters. And I have hopefully made the case for those qualities that can be learned from learning about various dog breeds. Here is a fairly succinct summary of all the pertinent main points covered in the book.

Leaders Should Be Courageous and Communicate Well

These two qualities, that is, courage and communication are indispensable in leaders. How can a leader inspire his or her followers if they demonstrably lack courage? It's just not possible to be inspirational and be cowardly. Intestinal fortitude is the order of the day, and the list of dogs I used in the courage chapter ought to teach us all the importance of being courageous.

Take the examples of the various livestock guardian dogs or the shepherd dogs discussed in that chapter—they lead fairly risky existences, always having to be watchful and present in the bitter cold or torrid heat, watching out for predators who are on the prowl to bag a meal, be it a sheep or a lamb. While in the corporate world, leaders don't necessarily have to brave the torrid heat or the tundraesque cold, they still have to assume the role of protector of the organization, and that job comes with a healthy pre-requirement of courage. A leader lacking courage is not going to be able to protect either the company or the employees. So, take on the mantle, and get a dash of courage into your bones and your decision-making—if a Komondor or a Kangal can brave the wolves of the wilderness to protect its flock, so too can a leader protect his or her "flock" and "organization" as well. All they need first is courage, to implement and carry out strategic decisions.

The communication aspect is another one that I have often thought (and expounded on in Chapter 3) is integral for leaders. If a leader cannot communicate well, then no matter how courageous or brilliant that person is, it will not be appreciated or comprehended. One needs to work on communicating all sorts of information to one's network of colleagues and followers—a leader who sits back and doesn't communicate, especially in times of crises, is probably going to have to leave after the crisis. When one considers

SETTER(ING) DOWN TO A CONCLUSION   131

dogs, one begins to realize that they are masterful in their communication ability, be it verbal or nonverbal, and they are even better at understanding people's communication. And of course, leaders should improve their skills when it comes to communicating bad news—in many corporate settings, bad news is delivered bluntly with no regard to how it may be received by the recipient. Leaders should work on delivering communication with empathy— sure it may be bad news, but there's no reason it has to be delivered badly is there? Deliver it professionally instead of yelling like an irate medieval town crier suffering from gout.

Often leaders need courage too to be able to communicate bad news. After all, there are plenty of times when bad news or disappointing news must be delivered, and it's important to take charge and deliver it yourself as a leader. This other now-retired CEO I knew would always make it a point to go in person to deliver bad news (especially when he was forced to take drastic strategic decisions and close down some factories, during a lean stretch in the early 2000s). He said that he owed that to his employees—that he would never condone what some other leaders did, by hiring some nameless faces to go deliver the bad news. No, he was the CEO, and he wanted them to know that he wasn't taking those decisions capriciously. I used this example back in Chapter 2, but it's such a great one that it warrants getting another mention. That leads to the next lesson for leaders.

Leaders Should (Be and) Establish a Climate of Kindness, Respect, and Gratitude

Every day, it appears that we witness and see acts of unkindness, so much that an act of kindness truly blows our minds away, and tends to go viral all over social media (even if reality isn't quite embedded in the viral "kind act"). That goes to show that people are rather craving kindness and respect in an increasingly unkind world. Leaders can do a lot to change that overall climate, even if it's on a small scale. For starters, they should go ahead and embed kindness, respect, and a sense of gratitude in their own demeanor and behavior. It would not do for leaders to bark about for kindness while being obnoxiously unkind or disrespectful themselves. That would be similar to talking the talk but not walking it. But a bigger benefit would accrue if leaders focus on creating organizational climates of respect, kindness, and gratitude.

This will not happen overnight, and it will not happen without a major culture change. But over time, steadily, it can and will happen. Think of it in terms of water dripping on solid rock—over time, those water droplets can shape the rock into something really different. Ditto with culture—it takes time to change, but it can change. All it needs is a determined leader to

132   LEARNING LEADERSHIP FROM DOGS

spearhead the change. Yes, there may be some mutinous employees who resist change, but that is inevitable. The task is to kindly yet firmly bring them on board (like a Collie being firm yet kind while bringing a recalcitrant sheep back into line), and well, if they don't wish to be on board, wish them luck and bid them adieu, as being committed to culture change means everyone has to be on board.

So, establishing a culture like that can take time, but the process itself is fairly straightforward. First, the leader should model the behavior and attitude they want their followers to demonstrate. A lot of people tend to imitate the behaviors of their leaders, as they understand that those behaviors are what is expected from them as well. This is where the authenticity part (the concept discussed in Chapter 4) comes in handy. If you are wanting change in your organization or group, then model that yourself. Second, create or tweak your policies to reflect that change, and make sure your middle management and human resources people know that change is afoot. For instance, kindness involves treating individuals with dignity, and gratitude means employees need to be thanked for their stellar performance. It may seem as if this is pretty basic stuff, but the reality is that a lot of leaders and a lot of organizations have been making merry avoiding these basics. Only when the culture of a place changes for the better, will the levels of trust improve throughout the organization.

Another CEO I know (this leader is still working) had a specific experience changing the culture in an organization. It took a while, but after the new culture was established, she found that all of the employees in the organization relished the new culture, and expressed to her how happy and grateful they were that she had orchestrated the culture shift, away from a previously ugly hypercompetitive place to a place of collaboration and kindness. She told me that the new culture operating in the company seemed to have made the place a lot more productive, and workplace accidents were way down. In many ways, this mirrors what a host of research studies have already found. So, while it may take some grueling thought behind it, it is well worth the effort to bring about a culture shift in the organization, to make the place a kinder and more respectful place.

Leaders Should Be Joyous, Resilient, and Improve Their Intelligence

With the previous chapters on joie de vivre, resilience, and intelligence; it goes without saying that leaders should absolutely improve their own levels of these attributes. While certainly, resilience and intelligence are straightforward enough to improve, the joy factor can be a bit different and

SETTER(ING) DOWN TO A CONCLUSION 133

difficult in comparison. This is primarily because of the lack of passion, and different personality types. A melancholic (the urge to drop a pun involving a sad Collie is quite high at this point, but one must resist!) individual isn't likely to suddenly turn into an exultant individual.

Being more joyous and allowing oneself to embrace joie de vivre in your life is a much more individualistic choice. One cannot just become joyous just because someone tells you to—the way to do so naturally is to carve out time for yourself to engage in and partake in activities that you enjoy doing. If going for hikes in the hills or mountains is what gives you joy, go do that. Take a break, and do the things that truly give you joy—make yourself self-aware about what makes you truly happy, and go do that. I can guarantee that if you do that, you will be forcing yourself to become more joyous and embrace joie de vivre. Oh, and if you go out walking or hiking, take your dog along, do.

In terms of intelligence, while we can't suddenly become Einstein-level geniuses, we should remember the old saying about old dogs not learning new tricks. I firmly believe that it is entirely possible to teach an old dog new tricks—our minds may not be as fresh as it was in our days of youth, but that doesn't mean that they've stopped working. It is absolutely possible to keep our mental acumen sharp, and the same holds even truer when it comes to emotional intelligence. We can always learn new information about how to read or manage diverse people. The key is to increase interactions with people, that's really the best way to improve your own emotional and social (or cultural) intelligence. Get out there, and mingle with people, regardless of whether you're a leader or not. You will be improving your leadership skills either way.

The resilience chapter ought to be pretty fresh in your minds (unless you're reading this book like a manga, then things may be a bit harder to comprehend). And that one too, the best way to increase resilience is to get into situations where the likelihood of failure is a little high. Only by failing, and then subsequently learning not to fail, can you improve your resilience. All of this goes hand in hand with intelligence too—the process of failing and then trying again with an improved plan will increase your levels of intelligence (all forms of intelligence too).

Final Thoughts and Summary

I guess, we're drawing to a close now, so I may as well discuss a bit about what led me to write a leadership book centered on dogs. I suppose, I have explained the dog link earlier in this chapter, let's explain the leadership link now. Over the past decade and a half, I have taught a variety of courses in leadership, across levels, that is, undergraduate, graduate, and doctoral levels, and have published a fair amount of research in journal articles. I have always felt that a lot of leadership knowledge that currently exists is written in tedious verbosity, which just isn't as fun for non-pompous types to understand. Wouldn't it be so much more fun to have books on leadership that are easier to process, and fun to read? In response to that thought, I first wrote a leadership book situated within the context of the Harry Potter world back in 2022.

That was fun, and there's an interesting pop-culture and leadership series, that the book was situated within (I'm writing another book in that series, that one is situated in the context of *Buffy the Vampire Slayer*).

I have always found it somewhat startling that not everyone knows about so many of the breeds available in our world. And with the rate at which trends are moving in current times, I am rather concerned that many of these breeds I've discussed in the book could be destined to extinction. That would be a terrible tragedy, and I do hope that when you consider a potential dog for yourself or for your family, you consider one of the breeds I've mentioned in the book. There's no need to get overly expensive designer pooches from puppy mills and pay thousands of dollars for qualities that don't really exist with any certitude of reliability, when you can get a well-established breed which has been bred for those specific qualities over several hundreds of years, in many instances.

So, essentially, the purpose of this book was to introduce you all to the various dog breeds out there and to also comment on what specific lessons leaders (and future leaders too) can take from those dogs. I do certainly hope that you have learned something useful from the book, and mostly enjoyed the journey from beginning to end. I certainly wish you all the best in your future endeavors and hope that you get a chance to live life to the fullest with your dogs and future dogs (regardless of whatever breed your dog may be!) The joie de vivre aspect is universal across all varieties of dogs! May you find your own joie de vivre in life—if you're having difficulty, then look to your dog and follow his or her lead. If you don't have a dog, then go get one! That will change your life (for the better!).

INDEX

Adaptive Leadership 23
Afghan Hound 94, 99–100
Airedale Terrier 82, 87
Akita 71, 76
Alaskan Malamute 23, 72–73, 75–76
American English Coonhound 122, 124
Anatolian Shepherd Dog 11, 16
Australian Cattle Dog (Blue/Red Heeler) 22, 27
Australian Shepherd 91, 99
Authentic Leadership 29–31, 33, 35–37
Azawakh 118, 124

Balanced Processing 31–33 (see also Authentic Leadership)
Basenji 22, 27
Basset Hound 60–61, 63
Beagle 25, 28
Bedlington Terrier 105, 111
Belgian Laekenois 13, 17 (see also Belgian Sheepdog; Belgian Tervuren)
Belgian Malinois 13–14, 16
Belgian Sheepdog 13, 17 (see also Belgian Laekenois; Belgian Tervuren)
Belgian Tervuren 13, 17 (see also Belgian Laekenois; Belgian Sheepdog)
Bernese Mountain Dog 68–69, 76
Bichon Frize 46, 97, 110
Black and Tan Coon Hound 122, 125
Black Russian Terrier 82, 86
Bloodhound 25, 57, 59, 62, 65
Bluetick Coon Hound 122, 125
Border Collies 23, 27, 30, 32
Borzoi 44, 60, 64
Boston Terrier 104, 111
Bouvier des Flanders 11, 16
Boxer 42–43, 49–50

Briard 95, 100
Broholmer 70, 76
Brussels Griffon 109, 112
Bull Terrier 104–5, 111
Bulldog 4, 9, 11–13, 16
Bullmastiff 121, 125

Cane Corso 58, 65
Cardigan Welsh Corgi 109, 112
Castro Laboreiro Dog 93, 100
Catahoula Leopard Dog 122–23, 126
Cavalier King Charles Spaniel 45, 51
Chihuahua 36, 38
Cognitive Intelligence 89–93, 95, 98–99
Coton de Tulear 45–46, 50–51

Dachshund 61–64, 69, 74
Dalmatian 109–12
Dandie Dinmont Terrier 74, 76, 80
Dobermann Pinscher 54–55, 63, 92
Dogo Argentino 57, 63–64
Dutch Shepherd 13–14, 17

Emotional Intelligence 46, 81, 89, 94–99
English Mastiff 35, 55, 57–58, 63
English Pointer 20–21, 26
English Setter 20–21, 27

Fila Brasileiro 56–58, 63–64
Fox Hound 117, 124
French Bulldog 30, 38

German Pointer 20, 26
German Shepherd 13, 16, 55, 61, 69, 92
Giant Schnauzer 82–83, 86–87
Golden Retriever 49, 51
Gordon Setter 20–21, 26
Grand Bleu de Gascogne 60, 62, 64, 122
Great Dane 56, 69–70, 75–76

136   LEARNING LEADERSHIP FROM DOGS

Greater Swiss Mountain Dog 69, 76
Greyhound 116–17, 123–24

Hungarian Vizsla 122, 125

Indian Spitz 92–93, 99
Irish Setter 20–21, 26
Irish Wolfhound 43–44, 50, 69, 73

Jack/Parson Russell Terrier 106, 112

Kangal 11, 16, 130
Keeshond 93, 99
Kerry Blue Terrier 80–81, 86
King Charles Spaniels 45, 50–51
Komondor 10, 16, 130

Labrador Retriever 30–31, 38
Leonberger 83, 87

Miniature Schnauzer 83, 87
Moral Perspective 30, 33–34
Mudhol Hound 117, 123–24

Neapolitan Mastiff 56, 63
New Guinea Singing Dog 23, 27
Newfoundland 31, 42, 49–50, 83

Otterhound 4, 33–34, 37, 47, 59, 82

Papillon 96–97, 99–100
Path-Goal Leadership 20
Pekingese 36, 105–6, 111
Pembroke Welsh Corgi 109, 111–12
Portuguese Podengo 108, 112
Portuguese Water Dog 108, 112

Presa Canario 57–58, 64
Psychological Capital 115–16
Pug 35–37, 55

Rampur Greyhound 117, 124
Redbone Coonhound 122, 126
Relational Transparency 30, 35–36
Rhodesian Ridgeback 120–21, 124
Rottweiler 54–55, 63
Rough Collie 4, 31–32, 37, 92

Saint Bernard 11–12, 16, 92
Saluki 118, 123–24
Samoyed 22, 27
Schipperke 96, 100
Scottish Deerhound 108, 111–12
Scottish Terrier 121, 123, 125
Shetland Sheepdog 92, 99
Shiba Inu 5, 94, 100
Siberian Husky 71–72, 75–76
Sloughi 118, 124
Smooth Collie 32, 37
Staffordshire Bull Terrier 58, 81, 86, 104
Standard Poodle 24, 27, 89, 93
Standard Schnauzer 83, 86

Tibetan Mastiff 2, 123, 126
Tosa Inu 57, 64, 80

Walker Treeing Coonhound 122, 125
Weimaraner 122, 125
West Highland White Terrier 121, 125
Wheaten Terrier 73, 75–76
Wire Fox Terrier 97–100

www.ingramcontent.com/pod-product-compliance
Lightning Source LLC
Jackson TN
JSHW020200100125
76879JS00001B/2